PENGUIN

100 THINGS EVERYONE ELSE IS WRONG ABOUT

MIKE RICHARDS is the host of the highest rated show on TSN 1050, the marquee morning-drive program *Mike Richards in the Morning*, which has become one of the fastest growing morning shows in Toronto. Outspoken and always entertaining, Richards is one of Canada's top radio interviewers, having sat down with some of the biggest names in sports, entertainment, and the world at large, including Prime Minister Stephen Harper, former Toronto Maple Leafs captain Mats Sundin, boxing legend George Chuvalo, Super Bowl champion quarterback and CFL standout Joe Theismann, and comedians such as Larry the Cable Guy, Jeremy Hotz, Sean Cullen, and Andy Kindler. Amazingly, he is never wrong.

MIKE RICHARDS

100 THINGS EVERYONE ELSE IS WRONG ABOUT

PENGUIN
an imprint of Penguin Canada Books Inc., a Penguin Random House Company

Published by the Penguin Group
Penguin Canada Books Inc., 90 Eglinton Avenue East, Suite 700, Toronto, Ontario, Canada M4P 2Y3

Penguin Group (USA) LLC, 375 Hudson Street, New York, New York 10014, U.S.A.
Penguin Books Ltd, 80 Strand, London WC2R 0RL, England
Penguin Ireland, 25 St Stephen's Green, Dublin 2, Ireland (a division of Penguin Books Ltd)
Penguin Group (Australia), 707 Collins Street, Melbourne, Victoria 3008, Australia
(a division of Pearson Australia Group Pty Ltd)
Penguin Books India Pvt Ltd, 11 Community Centre, Panchsheel Park, New Delhi – 110 017, India
Penguin Group (NZ), 67 Apollo Drive, Rosedale, Auckland 0632, New Zealand
(a division of Pearson New Zealand Ltd)
Penguin Books (South Africa) (Pty) Ltd, 24 Sturdee Avenue, Rosebank, Johannesburg 2196, South Africa

Penguin Books Ltd, Registered Offices: 80 Strand, London WC2R 0RL, England

First published 2014

1 2 3 4 5 6 7 8 9 10 (RRD)

Manufactured in the U.S.A.

LIBRARY AND ARCHIVES CANADA CATALOGUING IN PUBLICATION

Richards, Mike, 1963–, author
100 things everyone else is wrong about / Mike Richards.

ISBN 978-0-14-319103-2 (pbk.)

1. Richards, Mike, 1963– —Anecdotes. 2. Sports—Anecdotes.
3. Sportscasters—Canada—Anecdotes. 4. Radio broadcasters—
Canada—Anecdotes. I. Title. II. Title: One hundred things everyone
else is wrong about.

GV742.42.R532A3 2014 070.4'49796092 C2014-904431-3

---

eBook ISBN 978-0-14-319307-4

Visit the Penguin Canada website at **www.penguin.ca**

Special and corporate bulk purchase rates available; please see
www.penguin.ca/corporatesales or call 1-800-810-3104

TO MY WIFE, LINDA, AND
TO MY SON, JORDAN—
THE TWO BEST PARTS OF ME

CONTENTS

INTRODUCTION

Dear Reader,

You know, you don't get to do my job unless you are *absolutely* sure about one thing.

You have to be crystal clear that *you are right.*

Lucky for me, I am.

Unfortunately, this sometimes means that other people are wrong. Unfortunately for them, I mean. It's not a problem for me at all. In fact, I find the experience of being right all the time quite enjoyable.

I'm not sure how I'd enjoy being wrong. I imagine I'd hate it. That's why I wrote this book—so that other people don't have to be wrong. If you read it, and pay close attention, you can be confident that there will be at least a hundred ways in which you can expect to be right.

That's got to be pretty encouraging, right?

You may ask, but Mike, you are already correct on a daily

basis on both radio and television. Why do you need to write a book?

Good question. Happy to answer it.

You see, it sometimes bothers me that each day, I spend hours saying things that I know to be right, only to realize that they *may* be forgotten one day. It is also a source of great pain to me that those who are not listening or watching each morning will never know how right I was. People who slept in that day, for example. Or maybe people whose radios weren't working.

In any case, with this book, I have solved both problems. Now, one hundred of the things I am right about have been recorded *forever*. To tell you the truth, I really don't mind this immortality. And, if your radio wasn't working this morning, don't worry. Plus, writing a book is one more way to be right, and I knew I would enjoy that. Some people think books are boring. Well, those people are wrong. (I'll throw that one in for free. That's number 101.)

Look, life can be complicated. There are many things we have to keep in mind as we make our way in this world. Things like sports. Things like gambling. Things like beautiful women. Surrounding it all are the larger questions like, "What should I have to drink?" Am I right? (Of course I am.)

But what you hold in your hands is a carefully compiled list of pure rightness that will help answer these questions. So go ahead: Pour yourself a little something. Now, turn the page in full confidence that you will never have to be wrong about any of these hundred things.

You're welcome.

Mike in Toronto, 2014

1 *EVERYBODY ENJOYS A VEGAN*

Who are these people and what planet did they come from? Is it the same planet Spock is from? Look, I don't even understand a vegetarian, but these veganites don't eat eggs or whipped cream? So no meat and no cake? I guess the Keg on your birthday is out.

What a terrible life decision. "But Mike, you'll live a healthier and longer life!" Really? Because I've been to small Italian villages where the people eat nothing but what the earth has given them, including delicious smoked meats, cheeses, lamb, pastas (made with eggs), breads, desserts, wine—and these people live into their thousands, smoking unfiltered cigarettes the whole time. I swear, the average age of the people who live in Villalago in the Abruzzo is 289. I'd love to hear the mangiacake who sits down for a beautiful dinner on a Sunday afternoon while the gorgeous prosciutto, grilled lamb, homemade pasta, breads, *cozze*, and *vino rosso* are laid on the table, and says, "Excuse me, do you have anything vegan?" "*Cosa*?" "Vegan?" "Vaticano? No. The Pope is a no here."

No hamburgers, steak, pork chops, or chicken fried steak? No osso buco, pulled pork, muffins, cupcakes, grilled-cheese sandwiches with bacon, corned beef on rye, or lobster? Why would you want to live? If you want to live that life so you can live longer, what are you going to achieve? World's most boring person? And don't give me the "Well, the substitutes that are made today mean that you can't tell the difference between fake bacon (fakin') or real bacon." If you can't tell the difference (and you can), why are you trying to emulate the evil meat, complete with taste, in the first place? Because you're a loser, that's why.

Be gone, vegans. We don't need your kind. According to the Book of Carnivore, Chapter 16, verse 4: "*And Michael did come down from the Foothills and through the Valley of the Bow. And, following from the words of the Burning Barrel, the Colonel sayeth to him, 'Strike down those of the fake bacon, cake, and beef. For they are the unnatural ones, who shunneth the Colonel, the Clown, and the Keg. Let the multitudes find salvation in baked goods, meat sauces, and Dairy Queen Frozen Treats. Do not be fooled by their imitations, for they are the Devil.' Michael took heed of the Colonel's words and packed his bag with only eleven herbs and spices and a single meatball from Subway sub and travelled to the City of Vegan.*

Michael was met at the city walls by those dressed in sandals and thick-rimmed glasses. 'Hey, friend, why not try our pizza, macaroni and cheese, or double-chocolate smoothie?'

Michael shouted, 'I will not be tempted by that which is not real. Open your city walls and let my people go!'

'No, we will not,' responded the King of the Vegans, whose name was Pretentious.

'Go back from where you came!' Michael sayeth again. 'I will ask one more time: Let my people go, for the Kingdom of the Colonel is for all, including snack packs, barrels, buckets, and the twenty-piece Family Feast.'

'No, you barbarian! The people stay and will hunger no more with our Raw Tuscan Kale Salad and Baked Quinoa Patties!' With that, Michael put his hand in his bag, and took thence the meatball, and slung it and smote the Veganite in his forehead and Pretentious fell upon his face unto the earth. Michael prevailed over the Veganite and slew him with no sword but that of the power of real food. Here endeth the lesson."

What more can I say? It's in the Good Book.

2 *BASKETBALL IS LAME BECAUSE THERE IS NO HITTING*

For some people in the world, there is only one sport: hockey. If you know any of these people, you know that they love hitting. (And fighting.)

If you think hitting is all there is to sports, you probably don't like basketball.

And if you're a meathead, you probably like announcing that things you don't like totally suck.

(Notice how I did that? If you disagree with me, you're a closed-minded meathead.)

Well, I'm sorry, meathead. Basketball is awesome.

What's so good about hoops? How about everything? When I look at certain sports, I break down what skills it takes to play and what skills it takes to play it *well.* Basketball encompasses almost every element of athletics: running, passing, jumping, hand–eye coordination, mind games, strength, and, most importantly, problem solving on the fly. It is also one of the best games for coaching tactics. You're constantly reading the opposition and adjusting.

A true test of natural athleticism: Throw a guy a basketball. When I was a kid attending hockey schools in the summer, if I wanted to know who the real athletes were, I'd just wait until the basketballs came out during breaks from the ice. Does the gorilla beside you dribble the ball like Martin Short? Does he chuck the ball at another kid's head? (It was a hockey school, remember, so there was a lot of that.) Or does he smoothly dribble the ball like he's done it a million times, and look to pass it to someone with a form that doesn't resemble skipping rocks or swimming the breast stroke? Hint: There's your athlete.

Basketball is pure competition, man to man. It's just you and LeBron (okay, maybe one guy's got more expensive shoes). No looking down at your golf club and frowning because your driver is two years old. No complaining about the flex in your new composite stick or the radius on your new blades. No complaining because the other team has weird dimensions in their ballpark, including a surprise incline in centre field. (Yes, Minute Maid Park in Houston, I'm talking about you. Oh yeah, and the flagpole that sits in the middle of the incline? Great idea. I'm surprised more parks don't have that.) In basketball, one ball, ten guys, one regulation court, and a net that is ten feet off the ground: Now go play.

I will always argue that the best athlete Canada has ever produced is Steve Nash. It's true that Canada is a hockey nation. I get that. And when you have a name like Wayne Gretzky, who has won nearly everything possible in his sport, how can you not hang the "Canada's greatest athlete" medal around his neck? Well, what did you expect? Of course, Canada produced the best hockey player ever. Seriously, what other country was going to do it? But a white kid, born in Johannesburg to a Welsh mother and an English father, growing up in Victoria, playing mostly soccer, and then going to Santa Clara University ... *that* guy would become a winner of back-to-back MVPs in the NBA?

How popular is basketball? Over 450 million people play it around the planet. There are 733 professional leagues in the world. Looked at an NBA roster lately? You need to speak about 27 languages to call a time out. Remember the dominance of the original U.S. Dream Team? Those days are gone, and the level of basketball has increased greatly around the world in the last 25 years. Small kids can play it, and those of us broaching "over-the-hill" can still have fun in pickup leagues.

They say you can tell what kind of person a guy really is by the way he treats a waiter. I'd add another test: You can always tell which guy in the office never played a team sport. How's it going, Selfish Stan? I always hear of these team meetings where companies get together with their staff, go to a lakeside resort, and share ideas (sorry, I mean "blue sky"). Forget that! You want Stan to play along, put him on the basketball court! No long weekend in Muskoka or Banff at a million dollars a day. Rent a court for twenty bucks and pass Stan the ball! If the running doesn't kill him, the ridicule from other staff members about Stan in shorts will.

Basketball is the great equalizer—well, that and booze, but that's another chapter.

3 *GUYS NEED BETTER MOVIES*

Very often I hear from people (well, women actually) that guy movies are "stupid" and perhaps "not very realistic." Yeah, we know. We saw *Commando*—the one where Arnold Schwarzenegger takes on an entire army on some imaginary Latin American island, saves his daughter Alyssa Milano, and defeats an evil dictator played by "Nick Tortelli" from *Cheers*. All by himself, naturally. Arnold comes to no harm, he doesn't get one scratch, and at one point he's able to defend himself by throwing a circular saw blade Frisbee-style and severing a guy's head. All in one afternoon … maybe a couple of hours.

So, does anyone think we want *realistic*?

Clearly not.

Do we want *awesome*?

Why, yes, we do. Thank you.

Guns, explosions, scantily clad women, and cheeseball lines … God I love it! Charles Bronson, Gerard Butler, Arnold, Jason Statham, Snake Plissken, and Steven Seagal. Would you spend a night watching these guys? How about a hungover afternoon? I've done both, and I can recommend each.

And this genre will never get tired for the male, testosterone-driven, all-bad-guys-must-die, caveman mentality all men have. And trust me, we all have it. Don't believe me? Look at the typical scrawny IT guy—he's computer savvy, is always polite to the people in the office, has that "too bad he can't find the right girl" vibe, and is sort of the nice-guys-finish-last type—you think he doesn't fall into this category? Who do you think makes the special effects and robotic monsters for pretty much every movie of this entire genre? Who invented the video games where flesh-eating Nazi zombies are blown away by machine gun–toting hookers? The gore gene exists in every male, and it arouses our imaginary need to conquer, destroy, and protect the weak, while at the same time getting the gorgeous Latina, bikini-model gymnast on a seemingly unending quest for lovemaking. (Okay, that last part was my particular thing.)

How about movies like *Hostel* or *Saw*? Are they too much to handle? Yes, if you're a pussy. Suck it up. You know the bad guys will get it eventually, although you do have to wade through some gore to get to their swan song. I mean, taking a teenage girl and sticking a blowtorch in her ocular cavity—that's just not called for! Severing a young man's Achilles tendon with surgical scissors while wearing a Minotaur mask and rubber coveralls—well, that's definitely offside! But revenge is on its way, and it's gonna be sweet! (Except for burnt-out-eye girl, who sees her reflection in a window, freaks out, and then jumps in front of a train and gets squashed.)

The only trend that I'm not big on that is very popular over the last fifteen years or so is that sometimes the bad guy wins. I hate this. You know why? It's too realistic. In real life, we know that the bad guy does sometimes win. All too often, in fact. But movies are supposed to be an escape from the harshness of reality—if I wanted to see reality, I'd watch reality!

The modern filmmaker wants more reality, to be less predictable, and therefore will have an ending reflecting the mores of current society. I say no! If the Green Goblin tries to kill Kirsten Dunst, then I'm sorry, Willem Dafoe, you gotta die.

So leave the format alone. It's perfect. Give me the cheesy lines, too: "He's just letting off a little steam," "Go ahead, make my day," or "Get off my plane!" Which reminds me, the best movies are also educational and provide lessons to pass on to the kids in your life.

So next time you see a movie with knife fights, stomachs exploding with baby aliens, or some zombie-head chopping, remember that it's making you a better person. And isn't that more important than reality? So, as Bruce Campbell in *Army of Darkness* would tell you, "First you wanna kill me, now you wanna kiss me. Blow."

4 *TALKING STATS IS FUN!*

Hockey used to be pretty much nerd-free.

That's because the game didn't *really* have stats. Basically, you kept track of the score and a guy's penalty minutes (interestingly, hockey is a sport in which players are admired for hurting their team—it's weird, isn't it, that guys get props for big PIM numbers?), and you were good. The rest was just watching the game and talking about intangibles: momentum, style, confidence.

Maybe that made it too easy to be an expert. Because somewhere along the way, hockey got stats. I mean, serious stats. Now we are discouraged from having an opinion on whether, say, Mikhail Grabovski should be signed as a free agent unless we know Grabo's Corsi number. What's his Corsi number you ask? Why, it's the sum of all shots directed by the player toward the other team's net (shots on goal, missed shots, and blocked shots), minus the sum of all shots directed by the opposition toward the player's net. What's Fenwick Close, you ask, once you have subtracted all the shots from opposing teams (and come up with a fairly large number)? It's like Corsi, you see, except without counting blocked shots. And only when the game is close. Or tied.

Having fun yet?

I know talking statistics has its place. It provides context. It backs up your hunches. The numbers themselves can support a reason why a play turned out the way it did, or why a player was successful in a given scenario. These things I understand, as it is a part of what I have done almost every day for the last, oh, say, twenty years. But, not for one second am I chatting about faceoff percentages, right-handed vs. left-handed pitchers, field turf vs. grass, or lottery draft odds and passing it off as FUN!

Numbers aren't fun; they are math and I failed math for a thousand years and I'm not going back! (You see, I don't believe if you added up my years of education, it would actually equal a thousand years, but this merely highlights my mathematical futility.)

Some guys love stats because they love numbers, and to these people, numbers represent perfection and logic. I like the human element of sports, which is the opposite of perfection. Humans make mistakes, and mistakes make drama. Is there a statistic out there that meaningfully captures the bug-eyed astonishment of millions of fans at the opening snap that sailed over Peyton Manning's head in Super Bowl XLVIII? *That* is sports.

Many of the most memorable sporting moments in history have come down to the miscalculation of others at the most crucial moment in a game. In fact, a huge part of sports is trying to force your opponent into just such an error. Part of it is deliberately causing a bit of chaos. A huge part of it is just going with your gut, right or wrong. Sometimes the game turns on a missed call, or a bit of luck. And sometimes teams create their own fatal mistake by playing the percentages. It's that kind of thinking that sends Ray Bourque out to take a penalty shot against Dominik Hasek, while Wayne Gretzky is left sitting on the bench. The Great One's stats in penalty shots weren't all that great, you see. How about that, stats lover? Yeah, that's right: Don't be predictable and play it safe because that's what the numbers are telling you.

The stats will give only part of the story. The real narrative of sports is the personalities and the triumphs of those who played. You want to argue numbers: Become a mathlete. Do you remember the race about who deserved to be the Heisman Trophy winner in 1984 based on a compilation of stats, or do you remember Doug Flutie's Hail Mary pass to Gerard Phelan in the rain on the last play of a Boston College game that season? The story to me is about the athletes, not the numbers.

Ever hear two baseball freaks talk about stats when it comes to Hall of Fame inductions? I would like to sit them in a rickety old cabin, held up by stilts just over a swamp, have them sit at a table with a gun ... and every time they bring up an argument about why a certain baseball player's numbers are better than another's, I want a Viet Cong guard to slam down his hand on the table and yell, "Mau!"

Championships are never cherished because of the numbers and statistics of the game, but because of the drama that unfolded to allow legends to hoist a trophy. I remember the 1986 Grey Cup between my beloved Tiger-Cats and the always-hated Edmonton Eskimos. It was in Vancouver, and the Ticats were huge underdogs. Guess what? Hamilton destroyed Edmonton. I couldn't tell you one stat about the game, but I do remember the Eskimo quarterbacks being sacked about two thousand times and I believe Paul Osbaldiston kicked sixty field goals. Final score:

Hamilton 39, Edmonton 15. I remember walking into 1050 CHUM, as I had to work that night, complete with painted face and balloons pinned right to my Ticats jersey (Chuck Ealey, of course). Greatest night ever, and to this date, I never need to know about the stats, because—honestly—if that game were based on statistics before the kickoff, Hamilton was supposed to get killed by the Eskies.

So argue all you want about stats, but you won't find me in that conversation for long. If you're looking for me, I'm the one in the corner, wearing a number 16 Ticats jersey with the balloons pinned on, glaring wide-eyed into space, and forever envisioning Grover Covington and Ben Zambiasi destroying the team in green.

Time for a drink.

5 *EVERYBODY KNOWS WHAT CALGARY IS*

I thought I did. Then I moved there and, of course, my life has never been the same since. People in Canada have a perception of certain elements of Calgary: cowboy hats, the Stampede, the Flames, the Stampeders, and people who say, "Yahooooo!" or "Yee-Haw!" (Be careful which one you say: One is wrong.) And none of these perceptions are out of place, but if you think that's all Calgary is, you're wrong. Everybody should be lucky enough to live in that city for at least one year of their life. The heart, the friendliness, and the drive of people are unlike any place else I have ever experienced. If you've never felt like you've had a hometown in your life … then do I have a place for you!

When I worked in Toronto, I would travel to see my good friend Gerry Forbes, the King of Calgary radio, and quite honestly one of the greatest people I've known, and he would show me his town. I realized very quickly it was a town—city by population, town by the feel because of its people. We'd go to a Flames game and for the first time I saw the Sea of Red. And let me tell you first-hand, everybody—and I mean *everybody*, be they accountants, lawyers, oil and gas millionaires, or hipsters—wears the team sweater, and not the cheapos either. The Flames score and real flames flare up, so hot you can feel the heat on your face! What?! And they love their team. The players are a part of the community. Go to a hot dog stand and then-captain Jarome Iginla would pass you the ketchup … and then ask how your family is doing. Unbelievable.

Going to a Stamps game is very similar, and they are a knowledgeable football town. You bundle up, snuggle with a Calgary cutie (and there are lots of those), have a cold one and a Spolumbo's sausage, and cheer for the Stamps. Walk out of McMahon Stadium—that's right, walk—with thousands of people, stopping off at your favourite after-place, and warm up with some of the nicest people, most of whom you're meeting for the first time. It's what a football experience is supposed to be. If you haven't been in a U.S. college town on game day, this is very close to that feeling and one of the best days you'll ever have.

Calgarians' grassroots support of amateur sports is fantastic (actually, that goes for the entire province). Coaching football at St. Mary's High School has been, and still is, the greatest experience I have ever had. A man who I call a friend but is more of a brother to me, Vini Sciore, brought a vibrancy into my life that I don't know if I ever had before. He is a born-and-raised Calgarian, and is typical of the amazing individuals who coach, teach, raise their families, and spend countless hours volunteering for every sport or cause that makes the city better. I miss him every day of my life.

The way that I was treated in Calgary, I wish I could give just a day of that to everyone so they could feel what it is like. The warmth of those who lived in the outskirts, the kindness I was shown by the people of Lethbridge (Stewball and Jeremy will be my friends 'til death), and the sense of community that I had never felt so strongly have made me a better person.

There is also a tremendous sense of courage when it comes to business ventures. It's tough to put your finger on it, but Calgarians seem to be willing to try anything, with some of the greatest enthusiasm I have ever seen. It doesn't surprise me that W. Brett Wilson comes from Calgary; he exudes the confidence and sense of fun that this city seems to generate.

The Calgary Flames Alumni: This is simply the finest and most fun organization I have ever been involved with. Colin Patterson, Perry Berezan, Jim Peplinski, and Lanny McDonald make that city special. Even those running the NHL team—the Flames have people like Rollie Cyr who are so giving and humble, after a while you start to think of them like family. I still do. And how can life not be good when the legendary Peter Maher is the voice of your hockey team? Nicest man on the planet.

So you think you know Calgary? You probably don't, but there are a thousand reasons to visit there at any time of year, including the great Calgary Stampede and my beloved chuckwagon races. But be forewarned: You may go for a vacation, but end up moving in.

6 BEING SAT OUT DURING A GAME IS A DEMOTION

Remember when Mike Babcock sat P.K. Subban in Sochi and everyone thought he was insane?

But then Team Canada won the gold medal and everyone thought he was a genius?

Turns out, sitting arguably the most talented player on the team, and officially the best defenceman in the NHL, is not a terrible idea after all. Sorry, P.K.—no hard feelings?

There shouldn't be. Because there are plenty of good reasons to sit a gifted player in the press box, as P.K. should know, having sat there before as a Montreal Canadien—despite being the team leader in ice time. Sometimes, to put the best team on the ice, you leave talent in the press box (and salary—hi there, Brad Richards).

Now, there are certainly circumstances in the NHL where being a healthy scratch is a reflection of a team just not wanting to play someone. Because they can't make that player shovel the parking lot, he ends up eating popcorn in the press box.

Some guys really do suck. But not very many of them play in the NHL.

The fact is that a lot of the time, guys are watching from the press box or standing on a sideline in order to learn the game. You see it better from a different angle. And it's often the most talented guys who get that opportunity. Notice it's the Leafs' most talented offensive defencemen, Jake Gardiner and Morgan Rielly, who get to watch the game from up high. And defencemen take longer to develop—Luke Schenn also was given the privilege of watching a number of Leaf games in a suit and tie. In Dallas this past season, Valeri Nichushkin, another raw talent (though a forward), got a fresh perspective. And it's not just young guys. Hard as it is to imagine, warhorse Jarome Iginla was scratched last season. Jarome *Iginla*. If Jarome Iginla can be scratched, *anybody* can be scratched.

The problem is that we have arrived at a time in our society where many believe that in sport, we are all winners. To a great extent, this is the way in which we have raised our children—everybody passes, nobody fails, everyone is special, and no one is ever forced to sit out or be left behind, as adversity has been all but eliminated. So, the idea that you are not being rewarded immediately must mean that somehow your worth to the team has lessened, and therefore sitting out is a "failure."

Since the advent of film and video, one of the greatest teaching techniques involves using media to visually identify the mistakes and tendencies of players. For a young player who is struggling, or a vet who may not understand a new system or scheme, the vantage point from the box or sideline is a tremendous tool. Sitting out can also serve another purpose: the settling down of emotions. Getting an athlete "on track" or "back on the rails" can be a tricky proposition. Sitting out too long can bring frustration or lower self-esteem; but if a player is brought back too soon, the message might get lost.

Maybe the wording itself brings the wrong connotations. It's sort of like the phrase, *sent down*. I've never liked it, simply because it sounds like the move itself is a demotion. It's funny, the team in the NHL that uses its farm system consistently to produce the highest quality of player, and has developed a reputation for having players enter the league when they are considered "overripe," is the Detroit Red Wings—and I hear no one refer to this system as a constant demotion or deterrent to winning championships. Ever heard of Martin Brodeur? Dominik Hasek? Maybe Curtis Joseph? All these guys spent the equivalent of more than a season bouncing between the AHL and the NHL. And things turned out pretty okay for them.

We should take a look at how we explain success at the grassroots level of sports. When we tell our children that in achieving success there may be moments of struggle and disappointment, we should also explain that when they are faced with adversity, it does not necessarily equate with failure but is simply part of the process in becoming successful.

It may seem odd to keep using examples that refer to our children, but remember this: The average age of a professional athlete is roughly 26 or 27, and plenty of even the biggest stars in the league are much younger than that. This just in: They're kids.

7 NORTH AMERICAN MEN LIKE TO DANCE

North American men like to be *where* dancing is. They like to be where dancing is *performed* and they like what it does to women. They don't hate dancing in *itself*.

But North American men don't want to dance.

For most men, dancing is our kryptonite—what liver was to Fonzie or the colour yellow for Green Lantern. (Yeah, get a load of the superhero who could be defeated by the colour of Ricky Martin's pants when he was in Menudo.) Fact is, we are definitely not willing to make any embarrassing sacrifice that may in any way damage our "cool." Thus, our patience—we will wait all night for the slow song.

Remember the high-school dance? Chatting with the rest of the boys, trying to act cool in front of the girls, who had no problem dancing together, you worried that you wouldn't get the "chick" you wanted if you didn't keep an eye on your prospective "prey." The careful positioning and posturing rivalled anything you would see on the National Geographic Channel. Eye contact carefully economized (too much and you look like a stalker; too little and you're not in the game). Timing painstakingly agonized over (don't look like you're competing with one of the other guys). And for God's sake, it better be a slow song.

The last song of every dance, in my era, was Led Zeppelin's "Stairway to Heaven." It was 8 minutes and 3 seconds of feely-feely good times. But wait, what happens at 6 minutes and 45 seconds? It's the answer to the question you've been waiting for all night! As Robert Plant wails, "And as we wind on down the road" and the tempo picks up, if she separates and goes into the fast-dance mode, you've blown it! Sorry, no necking for you! Ah, but if the groping continues, "He shoots and scores!" This to the average Canadian boy in the 1970s and '80s was as close to dancing as we could get.

It doesn't matter how often you go to the gym, what you bench press, how long you played linebacker in college or captained your junior hockey team: The moment your girlfriend drags you on the dance floor during a Caribbean vacation, because she wants to "salsa dance like everybody else," you become the biggest pussy on the planet. It doesn't help that you're surrounded by a lot of the Latino staff who are swivel hipped, tight panted, and look like they would all win on *Dancing with the Stars*.

YOU: Let's wait for a slow one.
HER: This is a slow one!
YOU: I wonder if they know "Stairway to Heaven" …
HER: Screw you, Tommy. I'm gonna find someone who will dance with me!
YOU: You better not ask Ramon from the Beach Bar, Ashley!
HER: That's exactly who I'm asking.

YOU: If you do, then don't come back to the room tonight!

HER: Maybe I won't!

YOU: Good!

HER: Good!

YOU: Great!

HER: I hope you die!

YOU: I hope you die!

(Well, maybe it just might be easier to take salsa lessons before you go. Just ignore that last scenario. I just made it up. Completely fabricated: no foundation in reality. Never happened to me.)

But as North American men, we love to be where the dancing is. And to be fair, inebriation at a club (and you know what I mean by *club*: the vaguely Euro, boom-chicka-boom-chicka-boom-chicka kind of joint) is fun. If there's a packed crowd, we'll all get on the dance floor then. But let's be honest: That's really not dancing. Dancing at a club is like a rhythmic prison riot where nobody escapes.

So, ladies, take pity on us North American males. We are trying, and if you happen to go on a vacation in the Dominican Republic or Cuba, go slow with us on the dance floor. Pretend, when we are dancing, that we don't look like we're being electrocuted, and if you're really feeling kind, ask the band to play a slow one. You know, like "Escalera al Cielo."

8 INTERNET PORN IS BAD

As I was researching for my show one morning, I saw an ad for Slut University. Hmmm, I thought, I'm not familiar with this school or the conference they play in. The banner said, "Come visit Slut University, where all the girls are whores!" Hmmm, I thought again, that seems to be a bit of a sweeping accusation, but on the other hand: good to know. Background information on SU: check!

That was that day I discovered that you can learn a lot of stuff that can help you in life if you would just open your eyes to the wisdom of the internet. And by "internet," I mean "pornography."

Since then, I have learned many things I have never come across in the public library. Did I previously know what a MILF is? No, I did not. Thank you, internet! And just look at what we have learned about MILFs and their habits: They like to dress up in suggestive clothes, walk aimlessly around shopping malls and gas stations, allow anyone with a video camera to sit down with them, and after five minutes of mindless and pointless conversation, let you take them back to their house or condo, and form a brief but intense friendship.

How about the inroads that have been made through exhaustive experiments in the area of porn transportation? Hitchhikers, teen hitchhikers, MILF hitchhikers, and all the various cultures of those who would get into a van with tattooed, mega-pierced, jobless men holding cameras, and still take a ride—these are the strides that have been made via the hard work of internet porn. "Wait a minute," you say, "what about larger forms of transportation, where there might be more than one girl looking for a lift?" Hello ... someone's forgetting about the Bang Bus. Sheeesh, do your homework.

You can also receive vocational insight from the internet to make sure you're going for the job that is suited to you. Career research might include an investigation of the Casting Couch, Fun Babysitter, Horn Hospital, Ass Accountant, Bad Teacher, Groundskeeper's Willie, and, for the legally minded, Lay Down Lawyer. What about earning a living on the high seas? Captain Stabbin' might be the vocational expert for you. All kinds of choices for the "real go-getter," all courtesy of internet porn!

Let's not forget the very helpful insights into the realities of modern relationships you can acquire thanks to the diligence of those who work so hard on internet porn. Marital strife affects people from all walks of life and from anywhere in the world. How about the significant strides made in the area of interrelationships from such revered sites as EuroBrideTryouts.com, Naughty Therapy, My Friend's Hot Mom, Married ... with Hormones, My Friend's Hot Sister, Good Grandma, and Wifey Like Wine?

By the way, I'll have to leave off with this chapter, as I have part-time jobs delivering pizzas, or sometimes working as a Jacuzzi repairman, or giving piano lessons to cheerleaders. Sure, they don't always have enough money to pay for my services, but I make other arrangements.

9 WINTER JUST MAKES YOU WANT TO GET OUT INTO THE FRESH AIR

Every New Year's Day, when reasonable people are watching the world juniors, other people huddle on the icy shores of frozen lakes, shivering in bathrobes and Speedos, then count down and splash together into the deadly, frigid water. Then they splash back out, wrap themselves in blankets while their teeth chatter dangerously. Then, I suppose, they go home. God knows what these masochists do when they get home. I won't guess.

Because they are masochists, right? The only reason to jump into an icy lake is that it's so obvious that no one would want to do it, you must be making a point. What that point is, I've never really tried to guess, because the most important thing here is that these people are admitting they don't want to jump in a lake, even as they jump in a lake.

Sounds crazy, right? Well, not as crazy as snowshoeing.

Why, you ask? Because the polar bear dippers at least know it's a bad idea to get cold when you could be inside watching

Canada beat Slovakia. Snowshoers seem to think that trudging through the cold is *fun*.

Snowshoeing isn't fun. It's just walking, except colder. Not that I'm anti-walking. Hey, I walk, too. But I don't tell myself, or others, that it's fun. Especially when it's cold outside.

I always find it funny when people start describing all the things they love to do during the wintertime. "I love, after a wonderful day of skiing down the mountains, that you get to lounge by the fireplace in the ski lodge, warming yourself up and sipping on a nice glass of brandy with family and friends ..." What a great story. By the way, when did this happen for you? Does it rhyme with "schnever"? Do you vacation a lot with Lord Snoddington? Seriously, the only people I know who sip brandy also clean my car windows under the Gardiner Expressway. Wintertime stories sound fantastic: tobogganing, cross-country skiing, roasting marshmallows, and skating while eating sugared plums—all wonderful memories that never happened. What is it about winter activities that makes people think they are inhabiting Norman Rockwell paintings?

"Oh, I love it when there is a bite in the air." Really? Because everyone I know hates it. You know what winter means to a lot of people? Mexico.

"I just love skidooing!" I say this phrase all the time. I talk about the power of the machine, the powdered forest trails, the rush of speed as we plunge through the snowdrifts. There is one problem with this frozen memory, however: It's never happened. Ever. I'm not saying I would never consider snowmobiling. But then it's, "Hey, who wants to go to Punta Cana?!"

Now, I've never gone ice fishing before, but from what I gather, this might be a little more realistic. Essentially, ice fishing is about guys escaping from their families; travelling with a group of other male familial refugees; and heading to some faraway hut, a warm comfortable man cave where they catch fish and drink until their judgment becomes questionable. In principle, I'm in! Screw the candied plums, the children with rosy cheeks, and Aunt Sally with her spiced cider: Daddy need drinky.

Some other less-than-fun activities that no one needs to do or suggest: hikes in the snow, making snowmen, collecting pine cones, carolling door to door, or any jobs having to do with maple syrup. All of these things (and especially snowshoeing) just sound like chores you would do to survive in, say, 1806. If the plane carrying your rugby team crashes in the Andes, and you have a choice between hiking through snowdrifts and eating your deceased teammates, maybe snowshoeing doesn't look quite as bad. (Mind you, if Guy Fieri were on that mountain, he might have told the survivors, "Dude, I love how you've prepared that human torso. The saltiness of the meat is balanced by the burn of the frostbite on the skin. That's some bang-on crispy human ass, bro!")

I know I will hear about the fun you can have making snow forts. This *is* true. The word *fort* is in there, so it implies warfare, which is something that piques the male interest. Ice-ball attacks and tackling children in the snow are very appealing, you've got me there. But you know what is even more appealing in February? A swim-up bar in Cancun. If you want a warm cosy cabin in the woods, surrounded by snowdrifts and stars, a giant stone fireplace with a bear-skin rug, just do what I do: Rent a movie called *Jenna Jameson's Magical Christmas Box.* She plays Mrs. Claus.

10 *THE GREY CUP IS IRRELEVANT*

Seriously. There are people who believe this.

I understand that there are haters out there who are anti-CFL no matter what. Fine. I can't pass a law forcing people to like the CFL. (Still, write to your MP.) You don't like it? Go ahead and watch badminton. But if you're trying to argue that the Grey Cup isn't a big deal in this country, I hope you're not the anchor on a debate team. (Is there such a thing in the world of debating? Anchor? I wouldn't know. I hear the term *debate team* and I think multiple wedgies and bad school recesses.) The television numbers for the Grey Cup game rival the biggest audience numbers in Canadian television. It's not just a draw, it's about as big as a draw can get in Canada.

Courtesy of TSN:

> According to BBM Canada, the 100th Grey Cup Game drew an average of 5.5 million viewers on TSN, making it the most watched CFL championship ever

> recorded on English-language television and overall, more than 13 million Canadians—or more than one in three Canadians—tuned in to watch some or all of the Sunday night final on TSN and RDS.

It is still the one truly Canadian celebration that just doesn't stop, even though arguments to the contrary sometimes make their way into conversation. I hear things like, "If the Blue Jays went to the World Series ..." Sure, no question. But when the Blue Jays haven't been in the World Series, what does the network draw nationally? Well, according to Sportsnet, they get 460,000 to a high of 726,000 viewers. These numbers were for Boston and St. Louis in 2013. Now, a single-game broadcast such as the Grey Cup is always going to draw a bigger number, not unlike the Super Bowl, which last year drew an average audience of 7.3 million viewers, according to CTV. Impressive, but the Grey Cup is still in that universe.

There's also a festival atmosphere to Grey Cup week that has just gotten bigger and bigger over the years. As embattled as the CFL has been in recent decades, and it is true that a generation of fans were lost during the hometown television blackout era (the 1980s), the CFL has a reputation today as the "fun league" whose championship game and the days leading up to it are a party. That is not lost on the younger fans. If you want to argue over its significance in Toronto, that is a separate issue, and one the league and the Toronto Argonauts continue to work on. (A new venue would be a welcome change, and considering the facelift that has been going on in stadiums across Canada, including the refurbishing of BC Place, the new Investors Group Field in Winnipeg, and the upcoming new facilities in Hamilton, Ottawa, and Regina, I would see this as a realistic endeavour.) But maybe the best thing the league can do is make sure the Grey Cup is held in Toronto whenever Saskatchewan represents the West. A crew of Roughrider fans ripping it up for a week straight might give Torontonians a better sense of what they're missing.

I can tell you, it's not just the boozing either. Sports is always about shared traditions and cheering for someone you have something in common with. That's why as long as there is a league where the guy who just made that leaping one-handed reception went to Concordia or Western or StFX, or where a passionate and loyal fan base will appreciate a good punt out of the end zone off a missed field goal, the Grey Cup will endure. It may not *always* be pretty. And yes, people may show up at games with watermelons on their heads. And if you, personally, don't like it, I guess all I can say is that you're missing out. But don't think for a minute that the rest of the country doesn't care. There is a pride on show in the third week of November that I wish carried through the whole year, and in many places, it does.

11 A GOOD OWNER GETS INVOLVED WITH THE TEAM

I once saw General Norman Schwarzkopf speak in Los Angeles at a radio-industry convention, where he was the keynote speaker. The theme was about organization. He got up and said, "It doesn't matter what goddamned business you're in. You don't put yourself in charge of a large group of men, let's say to put up tents, and then stand over each of their shoulders while they put up each one! You delegate the task and move on. And don't hire idiots. If they can't put up a tent, fire their ass."

The real problems seem to arise, though, when the guy who should be doing the firing is the idiot who can't put up the tent. You see where this is going. There may be some cases of an owner getting his hands dirty on a daily basis where it works out for the team, but it would be a rarity.

Mark Cuban of the Dallas Mavericks comes to mind. But his ability to make all the right business moves, keep a personal connection with players, and still allow his administrators and coaches to do their job is an anomaly. And even he can be a distraction for the players, chirping at the officials all game and earning fines from the league.

The best owners stay almost completely out of the mix, because they hire those who can make the right choices and decisions based on their expertise of that particular sport. That's how they got rich in the first place, right? Not by pitching tents, but by hiring the people who do. What I always find interesting is why certain owners feel they need to operate differently than the actual business that made them wealthy in the first place.

And wealthy and successful they are. From Arthur Blank of the Atlanta Falcons, co-founder of The Home Depot, to Pat Bowlen of the Denver Broncos, a lawyer from Edmonton whose family was into oil drilling, the money garnered by these individuals is staggering (in the billions). Jerry Jones is another oil tycoon, and he's worth almost $3 billion. Did becoming involved in every aspect of Jones Oil and Land Lease make him all that money? Probably did, and it should be mentioned that in the early '90s, Dallas won three Super Bowls. So what has happened since then? Jerry is the main attraction in Dallas. He is first; the team is second. Jimmy Johnson's personality used to be enough to offset Jones's. Now that he's gone, it's a circus. Is it a great business? The Cowboys are one of the most lucrative sports franchises in the world. But they will never win another championship under his watch.

Mike Ilitch: You almost don't need a qualifying sentence when you're that successful. Here goes, though ... for a start, he's the Little Caesars Pizza co-founder, but the Ilitch family also owns the Detroit Red Wings and the Detroit Tigers. When you look at the people Ilitch and company hire, and why, it's not hard to see why both these teams have so much success. The Red Wings and Tigers also practise patience and have the ability to grow their own talent from within. Those hired in the front office and to coach are a reflection of a philosophy that comes right from the top and probably carries over to those who purchase pencils: Ownership doesn't waver. (By the way, do they still make pencils?)

Who falls into the category of great owners who have an involvement with the team and yet manage to hire the right people and not get in the way? The late Jerry Buss of the Lakers was a trailblazer and an innovator and yet in his hiring practices built the kind of franchise that has become legendary and influential in the world of professional sport. He lived and breathed Lakers, yet the team ran itself, by the players they drafted and signed and the legendary coaches who ran the team.

It's tough in some cities where wealthy individuals will run their team like an expensive toy, but those owners are becoming rarer, as many sports franchises—especially in the NFL—cost the better part of a billion dollars. So listen up, wealthy owners: Make sure you trust those you hire, and when you spend the money, you need to spend it on a person who has the right resumé. It will allow you to date really young supermodels, collect expensive stamps, and drink bottles of wine that cost the same as your car. And remember this: "If they can't put up a tent, fire their ass."

12 A GUY HAS TO BE THE TOTAL PACKAGE TO GET GIRLS

I've always said that there are three things any guy needs to get a girl: be funny, be polite, and learn how to cook. If there had been room for thirteen commandments, these would have rounded out the list. (Though, to be honest, the first ten probably covered more important issues, and the insertion of "be funny" might have put an unwelcome spin on the coveting, the murdering, and that whole graven image thing. Ever notice that there is both a commandment forbidding adultery and another forbidding coveting thy neighbour's wife? Evidently, this was a point that needed to be driven home.) Most guys will beat themselves up, try too hard, or even worse, not try at all when it comes to landing a woman. So do you need to have the square jaw of a Brad Pitt, the charisma of a George Clooney, the money of a professional athlete—and still find time to sing in church with the blind? Oh, you'd do great, no question. You're picking up for sure at Earls. But let's try to keep our feet on the ground.

Women do like an attractive man, without a doubt, but some of the traits of the good guy will go a long way. Remember the show *Blind Date*? I used to watch that show all the time and was always stunned at just how badly some guys would blow it with incredible girls. It seemed that the guy who was always so in love with himself couldn't understand that he was annoying. Annoying and stupid—traits that most women despise.

DIMWIT ARROGANT GUY: Wanna see my abs? I can do three thousand crunches.
WOMAN FROM THE SHOW: No.
STUNNED LOSER, TAKING HIS SHIRT OFF IN A RESTAURANT: Hey, yo, look at this. You like?
WOMAN: You're gross. I'm leaving.
MEATHEAD: Bitch.

Be just a little funny. Let's face it, the friends you usually like to spend the most time with make you laugh the most. Why would a woman, no matter how attractive, not want to laugh just like you? Think Paul Rudd, not Pauly Shore. Impressions can be great! (Free Gift Number 1: A Victor Newman impersonation is a closer.) There is nothing better than watching a beautiful woman laughing at something you said—and no, this is not the kind of book that will proceed to tell you, "Now turn those laughs into moans!" Yeah, that's way too gross. Too much for sure. Or is it? Maybe ... well ... no, you're right. Yup, too much.

Being courteous is a must, and not just for trying to score points. There is something that is so refreshing about meeting someone who is well mannered. For most women, this is probably a rarity and therefore your politeness is a huge gold star in your attempt to win her over. (Free Gift Number 2: Always pull her chair out at a restaurant, allowing her to be seated first. It's a gentlemanly move, and you may get a glimpse down her top.) If you are ordering, please don't order for her; you're not in *Goodfellas*. Although, if you were in *Goodfellas*, wouldn't it be fun to be Henry Hill for just a short while? Especially when he pistol-whips that goof from across the street wearing the tennis sweater! Oh, where was I? Oh yeah, always be courteous and polite.

Most importantly, know how to cook! The new rock star of today is the chef. There is nothing more romantic than cooking something for your beautiful girl, preparing dinner right in front of her eyes. (Free Gift Number 3: Making seared scallops to perfection is nothing short of magical.) Have the right wine, and for God's sake, learn that, too, Goober! No more garbage plonk where you say, "Look, I got it for under $10 and it also came with this cool mini-bottle of bubble gum schnapps!" (Free Gift Number 4: Buy Prosecco.) And remember to put on the right music. (Free Gift Number 5: Play Earth, Wind & Fire's "That's the Way of the World.")

So don't worry, men: You have the power! Now get out there and find the woman of your dreams. (Free Gift Number 6: If you have no luck with any of these other gifts, rye and ginger—and don't stop until you start crying.)

13 MEETINGS ARE GOOD

Meetings are good for people who like to order in lunch. I hate them.

Nay, I despise them. There is a thought that gathering individuals in a room around a giant table will bring forth magical ideas. For the most part, it seems to be an exercise that convinces people they're "doing something," when in fact all they're doing is eating.

Every time a legitimate concern comes up, there will be someone who will state, "We need a meeting on this!" Translation: "I don't know what's going on. I'm a spare who is out of touch with the industry and I hope people notice my ties and not my fat ass." How about acting like a pro and figuring it out yourself? Now, I'm not averse to a meeting perhaps every few months to touch base and see if an individual needs support, or maybe there is a new idea, direction, or some information that previously wasn't available. But if someone says, "And there will be pizza," I'm out.

Ever see someone take notes at a meeting? What is this,

grade 7? Why don't I just get out my pencil crayons and ruler and underline the important parts so I can get a sticker? Have you ever seen someone who, after one hour of obvious blather, raises his hand to ask an even more obvious question? "So of the downward trend that we have seen, are we going to try and remedy the negative and move the results in a more positive direction?" If I had a blow dart, Stan would be getting it in the neck right now. What about the "I agree" guy? You know he's useless. If this were the movie *Hostel*, he would be one of the first guys to go.

Computers have now made possible video- and teleconferences, and those aren't bad. People may be sitting at different locations around the world and they can become as involved as they choose. I watched a full televised video conference on going to Ufa, Russia, for the world juniors, featuring a hot Russian girl named Olga, wearing no pants. (Note, I was pantless. She had pants.) It was awesome! The conference call meetings via speakerphone, however, are terrible. You can never hear the people you want and the person you don't want to hear from talks in a painfully loud and awkward voice, like a middle-aged adult trying to convince Gramps he has to live in a "special" home now.

Now, I know some companies have these weekend getaways. They sound bad. Do you have to bunk with weird Steve from accounting? What if he starts making noises in his bunk bed in the middle of the night? Will it look like *Full Metal Jacket* when Private Pyle gets beaten and he cries himself to sleep? I can't take that kind of pressure.

If you're going to have meetings, don't have a lot of them, and when you do, make them count—no ordering sandwiches, no pizza, and no soft drinks. Seriously, I've been to meetings and been offered a Fanta. Great, can't wait for Porno the Clown to come out with a bottle of Jergens. Just get to the point and everybody else shut up. If you want to see your co-workers outside of work, you will. Almost every person I have worked with closely is still a friend of mine. So be wary of the meeting. Someone may have a blow dart. And I'm looking at you, Stan.

14 *YOU CAN JOKE ABOUT ANYTHING*

I think you can joke about almost anything in life. I am someone who just doesn't take life, myself, or other people all that seriously, simply because the drain doesn't seem worth it. (And really, does life take *me* seriously?) You can tease guys about being cheap, lazy, slobby, snobby, philanderers, boozers—and maybe even chicken. (Careful with the last one: It's borderline to me. I might have to go Marty McFly on you.) The one thing I would never truly joke about is calling someone a cheater at golf.

Cheating at golf is a true reflection of character because it tells so much of what an individual is all about. Golf is a game where, for the most part, the honour system is in play. You are out there for hours with really only your own conscience and a couple of other guys present, but they are not actually counting your score, which is why after every hole they ask, "What did you get on that one?" The moment of truth. If you are playing with someone who you know has a reputation of skimming a few shots here and there, you start to watch, and to count, and, quite honestly, if that makes up your day, then you're golfing with the wrong guy. It's no longer fun.

I'm not talking about the casual round where, if it rolls into a divot or an unplayable lie, you're saying to another "ham and egger" to move the ball so you can get a play out of it. We're not on the PGA tour. And we are not talking about the "foot wedge" to move the ball five feet beyond a tree because you hit "into jail." That's all part of the fun when playing with friends. But there have to be some rules. And when someone claims that you are a cheater, that person is implying that you have no conscience when it comes to breaking rules. What you do in golf is what you will do in life. Does that sound cheesy? Too over the top? Trust me, it's true. It's about character.

I'll give you an example of how this once came into play. I don't profess to be a great golfer, or in reality even a golf lover. I was always a good athlete, so when I thought of golf as a kid, even when I worked at a golf course, I saw it as a pastime for people who weren't good at sports. Over the years, I've hacked around, and surprisingly, the older I get, the better my game has become, but as it is for many, it's really hit and miss. I've broken 80. Some years, I've consistently scored in the 80s and then there are days when I blow up so badly with my temper that I simply pick up the ball and drink. I believe that I am in a big category here. Strangely enough, when you play this way in best-ball tournaments, you can either be aided by better players when you're terrible, or you can carry the day if you're in the zone. When I've been on, I've won some pretty cool tournaments—my greatest achievement was winning the Calgary Flames Tournament, with the best bunch of booze-loving crazies ever. I love those guys.

But it was after winning a fun media tournament held at Calgary's Springbank Links, run by my good friend Kevin Heise, that the oddest thing happened to me.

One of the other media members, a guy I didn't know very well, said to me, "Oh yeah, Richards, we all know you cheated." At first, I brushed it off. Also, he was hammered. But, it bugged me. My demeanour changed. "Why would you say that?" Now on this day, my FAN 960 team was a player short, so they allowed us to rotate the extra shot among the three of us. I asked if that was what he was talking about. "No," he slurred, "you're just a cheater." Now, I don't like this hack, but we're in the public eye. I said, as I stood up in the bar, "Go ahead, call me a cheater again." On the wise suggestion from another media member, he ceased. I go a couple of years and never see this guy until one day I'm in a pub, he walks in, we exchange pleasantries, and he walks away. But as he is walking away from me, he turns, smiling, and says, "Still cheating at golf?" I was stunned. People at my table asked, "Who was that dick?" I replied, "A nobody. That's why you don't know who he is." All these years have gone by and it stills simmers beneath my skin. As I said, it's because of what I believe cheating in golf implies. I really hope we meet just one more time.

15 CHEERLEADERS AREN'T NECESSARY

Well, what in life is really necessary? Oxygen? Water? California Reds? Meat? Ice for drinks? These are all scientific facts, but what about cheerleaders? Would football games still go on if the scantily clad, aptly ripped, curvaceous cuties didn't tell us when to clap or, after 2, 4, 6, and 8, who they really appreciate?

Perhaps, but they indulge our weird male fantasy world, where we believe that the girls are there for us—literally. Somehow in our DNA—probably going back to Roman times, when the Caligulas of the world would throw lavish parties and then have "servants" please the guests because, well, that's what Caligula types did—we feel like we're frequenting the modern coliseum, complete with writhing girls, and that it's in some way the same thing. Don't believe me? Too far of a stretch? Have you ever had a conversation with "the boys" at a sporting event and when it came to the part about the cheerleaders, each of you "picked out" the girl you wanted? Yeah, yeah, that's right! The imaginary "look who I'm getting" part of the game! High-fives and deep laughing! More grapes, more wine, make the midgets fight, and which way to the vomitorium?

Maybe cheerleaders are not technically needed, but they are part of the atmosphere. It's also important to note that different kinds of cheerleading exist, each with a slightly differing role. For instance, U.S. college cheerleaders have perhaps the deepest roots in the origins of the cheer squad. Girl-next-door types with V-neck sweaters and little white socks—how can you get more wholesome than this? Rooting for the home team, names like Becky and Susie, pretty hair, ponytails, blondes at UCLA, brunettes at Penn State, and excited supporters watching from various American-as-apple-pie grandstands thinking one thing: *God*, I wanna take their clothes off in the back seat of a car! Actually, I saw a Peter North movie about this very topic. I thought it was very believable, but it could have used better writing.

NFL- or NBA-style cheerleaders are a different conversation. The pro style of cheerleading began with the famous Dallas Cowboys Cheerleaders, who in 1972 brought in Texie Waterman, a New York choreographer. Waterman recruited girls over the age of 18 and changed the uniforms to reflect a sexy, more mature image—the walls of garages, workshops, and boys' bedrooms were never the same again. The dancing and choreographed routines went from emanating a message like, "Come on, guys, let's score and win!" to "Just come, guys!" It seemed the names of the girls went from Sally and Betty to Sapphire and Monique. Trust me, no one's complaining. The Vegas-style sizzle is huge everywhere and the sophistication of some of the NBA dance teams wouldn't be out of place at the Mirage. I went to a Phoenix Suns game when Houston was in town. Sat behind about thirty

Chinese basketball fans who were quite thrilled when Yao Ming touched the ball, but when the Suns Dancers hit the floor, *boom!* Camera equipment of all kinds, squealing, pushing, and I think one guy had an X-ray machine. Yao Ming was big: Boobies were bigger.

Let's not be tough on the girls who dance, then. I'll be honest, judging from the ones I have met over the years, they are absolute dolls with personalities to match. My time spent with the Drill Crew of the Calgary Roughnecks in the National Lacrosse League might be some of my fondest memories from Western Canada. I can never thank them enough. The revamped Toronto Rock Cheerleaders are absolutely loved by their fans, and I adore them, too. So, clap for the girls, show them respect, and the atmosphere of the games will be better for it. Oh, and by the way, the girls know you "pick them out" and they're okay with it. God bless 'em!

16 COACHES AREN'T AS IMPORTANT IN THE PROS

I think it's safe to say that by the time a guy is making millions of dollars to play a sport, he no longer needs a grown-up to stand behind the bench to tell him what to do. Don Cherry likes to say that his job as coach of the Boston Bruins was to open the gate for Bobby Orr. Number 4 would take care of the rest.

Sounds reasonable. Ever see a bunch of pros play pickup? Awesome. The practices of the 1987 Canada Cup team are still legendary. Imagine Gretzky, Lemieux, Hawerchuk, and Coffey playing shinny. I don't care what sport it is, if you throw the best players out onto the ice, or the court, or the field, they are going to do something beautiful. And I'd bet that if your favourite team went into a game without a coach, they'd play their hearts out and put on a great show.

What they're not going to do is win.

Yes, talent and heart win games. That '87 Canada Cup team? In the second game of the final against the Russians, Mario had a hat trick. And all three goals were assisted by Number 99. No coach in the world can take credit for those two guys. But that's not the whole story.

That was an incredibly close series. As most of us know, the Soviets won the first game 6–5. Thanks to Wayne and Mario, Canada won the second 6–5. But in the third, Canada went down 3–0 before the third period was even half over. From then on it became a tactical battle, with Mike Keenan matching lines and grinding the Russians down. (Kind of a luxury to have Rick Tocchet, Dale Hawerchuk, and Brent Sutter as your grinders.) Finally, the stage was set for another game-winner by Lemieux and another 6–5 victory to take the tournament. So, yeah, that took grit and legendary levels of talent. But a victory that slim would never have come together without the tactics and adjustments that only a coach can make.

Need another example? Football is probably even more shaped by coaches than other sports. The New Orleans Saints of 2013 were a lot better than the Saints of 2012. Why? Did Drew Brees suddenly get better? Elite quarterbacks don't just "get better." For Brees, the return to dominance is a reflection of having an offensive "conductor" back in the fold. He didn't need more talent. He needed someone who speaks the incredibly complex offensive jargon; he needed a bit of analysis, a perspective from the sidelines, and maybe some fresh ideas. That's what allowed the offence to fly. Sean Payton's leadership and attitude were the key ingredients that were missing on the sidelines. So let's look at the differences between the roles of coaches at different levels.

In any sport, the early stages are about not only learning the game but also learning how to interact with other players and listen to the coaches. It is really the socialization of children that we are talking about, and therefore the role of the coach is pretty much the same as the role of the schoolteacher. To me, *coach* and *teacher* have always been the same word. So, if this trait exists in the early stages of coaching, why would it completely evaporate at higher levels? I would argue that as players mature, the degree of mentorship actually *increases*. Only the approach and the application are different.

In college sports, especially those schools with enormous programs, it is perceived that the coaches, because of the size of their rosters, no longer have the same kind of personal influence on their athletes than, say, a high-school coach. There is no question that there are certain coaches in NCAA who make an effort to be closer to their own players; and there are, of course, other coaches who see their players as just numbers in their system. Some coaches, upon recruiting players, will sit down in a family's home and tell them, "I'll look after your son." Some do mean it; others don't. It's up to the parents to do their due diligence in researching a school and a coach's reputation and resumé. The same goes for kids who are drafted in the OHL, QMJHL, and the WHL. Coaches at this level are motivating young men, still teaching a skill set, and for the most part still moulding them into fully functioning adults. Is all that really needed at the pro level?

If you have ever walked into a professional dressing room in any sport, you quickly realize there can be a divide in age groups, but for the most part it's a young man's universe. There is still a need for mentoring and a necessity for the coach to bring out the best in an individual—emotionally, athletically, or, for many, a growth in personal maturity. How can you tell if a coach is effective in any of these areas? Well, how many times do you hear about players being arrested for shooting guns in bars, committing domestic crimes, engaging in rampant drug use, or having police altercations and immediately you think of certain teams? Why is that? For the most part, the connection between player and coach has been lost. Now, I also don't think it's fair in this day and age to blame the coach entirely for every terrible decision a player makes. There are some tremendous coaches with excellent reputations who still get a bad apple. Attention, Aaron Hernandez!

There is also a feeling that pro coaches inherit players who have already acquired all the skill they need to be successful. If that were the case, no coaches would ever be fired. The fact is, coaches can waste talent by managing playing time and strategy ineffectively. Good coaches can bring the most out of a guy who maybe never had the chance to show the world what he had. Now imagine that you have to walk into a room full of millionaires and balance their numerous personality traits, skill levels, and egos. You have to monitor how they are interacting, and you need to analyze the play of the team full of (presumably well-coached) talented millionaires on the other side. You have to adjust to what that coach has done, and you have to adjust to his adjustments. I think attempting to be a successful pro coach in any sport might be one of the more difficult jobs in the world.

One thing that makes it easier is that even if fans don't know how important a coach's job is, the players know. Players want to win, and they know that the best way to get what they want is to listen up. (Notice how both teams start to play worse when the score in a game gets lopsided? That's because the players on the winning side know that they don't have to listen to attain victory, and the players on the losing team realize that no amount of listening is going to help.) And if you don't mind the firings; the constant moving; and the clashes with players, media, and owners, maybe this is a job for you. (But I doubt it.)

17 *PARENTS OF ATHLETES ARE ALWAYS A PROBLEM*

Don't you just hate parents who set aside their time and money to help their kids? They may do horrible things like get up early in the morning to *drive their kid somewhere*. Or maybe *volunteer*. Or, worst of all, they may *cheer loudly*. It's shocking, really. Someone needs to control these lunatics.

Look, I know it is common to talk about hockey parents in this country, and the stories are pretty much always bad. We all know the psychotic mother shrieking behind the glass and the red-faced father trying to start a fight with the other team's coach. Remember the story about the teenaged referee in Port Perry (a small town northeast of Toronto) who was assaulted by an angry parent in the parking lot—after a *novice* game? How about the assistant coach in Manitoba who left the bench to attack a ref and was afterward applauded by the head coach for "defending" a player? How about the two refs who had to lock themselves in a dressing room to get away from a threatening fan at a women's game in Barrie, Ontario?

Two things start to seem obvious:

1. You'd have to be crazy to be a ref.
2. Hockey parents are dangerous lunatics.

Wrong. (Well, number 2 is wrong; I can't comment on number 1.)

Think about it. This isn't a problem with hockey parents, it's a problem with *people*—some of whom happen to be hockey parents. Look, I'm not saying there isn't a percentage of nutters in every sport played, and some of them are going to be overbearing fathers or mothers. Out of thirty parents that may show up to see their kids play, what is a reasonable ratio of supportive and well-adjusted adults to those who are overzealous and live vicariously through their kids? Probably about the same as the ratio of decent people to jerks anywhere else in the world, I'd guess. Poorly behaved parents will always be present, but the way in which they are handled by the coaches and by the organization will dictate over time whether that number can be diminished.

Often overshadowed by crazy-hockey-parent hype are the truly excellent moms and dads who have made significant sacrifices to see their children grow and flourish in organized minor sports. They are the backbone of grassroots athletics, and the volunteers who show up on excruciatingly early Saturday mornings to work the time clock—not just because their son or daughter is on the team, but also because all the children of the community benefit from their hard work. And maybe that's just it. Having ground rules that make parents accountable not only for their children's actions but also for their own can force a parental responsibility that seems to be a great equalizer. There are ways in which turning the tide on problem parents has been achieved.

Parental code-of-conduct contracts are now very much a part of minor sports and the culture of fair play they are trying to create. Here is a portion from one of these contracts that is an excellent example of what is trying to be achieved: "As parents, it is absolutely essential that we give our coaching staff the respect and authority they deserve to run our team. Our coaches are hired for that purpose." Also, within these contracts, clear-cut behavioural guidelines are stipulated for parents:

> Our organization will not tolerate the following behaviour from parents:
>
> - Coaching your children at practice or during games; that is the coach's job
> - Interrupting or confronting the coaching staff during practice or games
> - Abusive language towards coaches, players, parents, officials, and your own children
> - Any behaviour that brings discredit or disruption to our players and our organization

Not every parent is equipped to immediately handle the pressure and expectation of what happens in organized sport. Some parents feel the anxiety more than the kids who are participating. Let's face it, sports can be intense. You don't have to be Mike Milbury to want to protect your son or daughter from some twerp you think has been giving your kid a rough ride. You've got a lot invested. That's part of what caring feels like.

Some people are going to go off the deep end. It's not as though there is anything preventing someone with poor impulse control from registering a child in minor hockey. But that's not a problem with hockey, or with parents.

But my experience has taught me that the majority of parents want to help all children succeed. Of the parents I have met at the highest levels of junior hockey whose sons have made the NHL, the number who are humble, grounded, and quite loving parents is always an incredibly stunning revelation. They rarely give off a vibe of elitism; instead, they tend to have a sense of pride in the accomplishments of their son, but they're not boastful. You have only to attend an entry draft in any city to see the families up close, and you realize that the hard work of great parenting has paid off. If you didn't know what the occasion was, you could mistake it for a graduation night, with parents strolling hand in hand, younger siblings running around with ice cream cones, and proud grandparents basking in the glow of the moment. Not all parents are a problem, and it's up to us to maintain a social safety net to change those who are.

18 BEAT REPORTERS CAN WRITE ANYTHING THEY LIKE

How would you like to score four goals in an NHL game? Think about it for a moment. Find the right words to describe the unique feeling of exultation a four-goal game might induce.

Done? Okay. Now, if it occurred to you that you might want to partially disrobe and masturbate in public to celebrate, well, that's kind of weird. But it's okay, too.

In any case, that's what Joe Thornton figured he would do if he had had the kind of night his rookie teammate Tomas Hertl enjoyed with the San Jose Sharks. Maybe you've spent some time in a dressing room yourself—in which case, Thornton's daydreaming might not sound as creepy as it would to, say, the chess club.

But the interesting thing about Thornton's comments was that they were part of a larger exchange, which featured a phrase athletes use pretty often when there are reporters around. "Have you ever played the game?" The other interesting thing is that athletes make off-colour jokes like Thornton's *all the time*, and they are pretty much never reported. Why? Because there is a code of ethics that ensures that both athletes and media respect each other. Something clearly went wrong the night Thornton was talking about his junk. What was it?

Well, the beat reporter, whose job it is to follow a team and its players for an entire season, doesn't have the easiest of jobs. As much as you like a sport, and in a lot of cases, the sport that they cover is a part of who they are, the demands of the schedule and the stress that comes with constantly maintaining relationships with team members must be extremely taxing. For the rest of us, the most travelling we do with a group of individuals (not our families) is a planned vacation with others. And for many, by the time the sixth day rolls around, you might be hoping that somehow one of the travelling companions gets caught in that dangerous undertow, or whatever it says in Spanish on those flags, so you never have to hear how special Tommy is at school and how he knows how to make toast at the age of 12. Can you imagine travelling with the same faces for eight months? So, yeah, athletes and reporters can get sick of each other.

But travel is just a necessary evil for what the job really entails: reporting an accurate assessment of what you deem as important to the fans. If you want to tell hockey fans about hockey, you'd better have an excellent if not outstanding knowledge of the game. And if you want to ask a millionaire athlete a tough question after a tough loss, you'd better have your facts straight, because he doesn't want to hear stupid questions. If he thinks the question is unfairly critical, or if he just doesn't like it, or if he doesn't like you, he's got a comeback ready. "Have you ever played the game?" It hits the reporter where it hurts—he's saying, you don't know what I know, and you never will.

Does a reporter have to have been an excellent athlete to accurately cover a sport, though? Well, the answer is clearly no, as some of the best sportswriters, including those in the various halls of fame, did not necessarily gain their insight based on athletic prowess. Elite sportswriters really have numerous talents to fall back on, including an understanding of the game, those who coach it, those who play it, and, most importantly, the ability to write an honest portrayal of events that is both accurate and entertaining. But it seems to me that the older reporters had something that I would call the "stink of the dressing room." Even though not athletes themselves, there was a fit to what their lives were about. It made for a mutual respect between them and players, coaches, managers, and owners based on an honest approach to what was written and what was not.

It seems that we have talked a lot about codes lately, with respect to how athletes react to each other regarding conduct. The same applies for those who cover the sport, and I would suggest it's a tougher juggling act than many might imagine. Can you go on air and rip a player about his defensive shortcomings and then stand right in front of him after practice the next morning and expect a friendly chat? What is it like to ask a coach about his decision to play someone who has perceived defensive shortcomings when perhaps the guy is standing right there? How does this affect a working relationship? It must be hard, but the good reporters are able to do it because they are consistent, honest, and accurate, without malice or personal vendetta. You treat the guys respectfully, and they respect you.

It goes both ways, though. Make fun of the guy holding the microphone, and there is at least a chance that he's going to print something you don't like. Especially if you're talking about fondling your junk in public.

Are mistakes made? I don't think anybody needed to know what Joe Thornton would do should he score four goals in a game—things that are said in the dressing room in jest that are meant for the people in the room only. In fact, it's usually a friendly gesture, a way for everyone to share a laugh. If it truly is newsworthy, follow up by asking for an official comment or asking, "Can I quote you?" In Joe Thornton's case, I'm sure the answer would have been no. Although any decent reporter would have had the follow-up question ready. The answer to "What would you do if you scored five goals?" might have been newsworthy.

19 ANYBODY CAN PLAY GOAL

There are 58 seconds left in the game, the score is 1–1 and your team just got a penalty. The 5-on-4 will now become a 6-on-4, with the whole season hanging in the balance depending on the outcome of the game. By the way, did I mention you're the goalie?

What is going through your head? Four things: a) "We're screwed"; b) "I hate the player who took that stupid penalty"; c) "Bring it on"; d) "I'll say the Lord's Prayer and promise repentance for all the things I've done, if He will just let the game go to overtime." If you picked c) and d), you're probably a goalie or should have been one. Oh, and that doesn't mean b) didn't cross your mind, but you'll let the coach deal with that one.

Not anybody can play net. Goalies are famously crazy. You can't talk to them before games, can't touch them, can't interrupt their routines. They love the pressure of being the last line of defence, but they don't necessarily handle it well. To have a mentality like that, it seems natural that there may be quirks to an individual who gravitates toward that kind of pressure. One trait can be the "nutty-superstitious-is-he-right-in-the-head?" kind of guy. How about this story, via *Hockey Buzz*: "Pelle Lindbergh wore the same orange T-shirt under his equipment each game. If it started to fall apart, he would have it sewn up, and it was never washed. Ever. In addition, the only thing he would drink during intermissions was a Swedish beverage called Pripps. Not only did it have to be that drink, but he could also only drink it if it had exactly two ice cubes in it, if it was given to him by a specific trainer, and would only take it from the trainer with his right hand."

Also, there are a percentage of those who play the position that are born-again Christians. This might make the most sense out of all the possible goalie traits. Who wouldn't want protection from a higher power when facing 100-mile-an-hour slapshots? Would you not seek divine strength when facing an angry Zdeno Chara after he storms into your crease with less than a minute to play in the game? (I know, I know, the David and Goliath reference and it just so happened that this very scenario occurred during the Maple Leafs' 2013 first-round collapse in Game 7, when Chara stormed into James Reimer's crease. [Reimer is a born-again Christian.] So what happened there? Simple: God is a Bruins fan.)

The goalie position has also changed significantly, where even the size of the athlete is nothing like it was twenty or thirty years ago. The average NHL goalie now is around 6'2" and 200-ish pounds, as opposed to the under-6-footers of days gone by. The proliferation of the likes of big puckstoppers like Mike Smith and Pekka Rinne, among a slew of other goalies, including Ben Bishop who is 6'7", has virtually eliminated from the NHL goalies who are 5'10" and under. I loved Mike Palmateer, Tony

Esposito, and Rogie Vachon, but if they tried out for an NHL team now, they'd get hired as Oompa Loompas, firing Kwinter wieners out of the "Make-the-Loudest-Noise" hot dog cannon.

Of course, there is another story of a goalie who also never changed his underclothing on a winning streak, with absolutely no thought of it seeing laundry; always dressed in the middle of the floor, regardless of the change-room capacity; didn't like his own teammates touching him before a game, especially head patting; and needed to eat two packages of black liquorice before every game. He was obsessive about his goals-against average and skated immediately off the ice after each game to figure out the math on dressing-room walls all across Ontario, in order to see exactly what his GAA was. His goalie coach one summer was Jacques Martin, and former NHL coach Mike Keenan sent him three invites to junior hockey teams in Ontario. Instead, that goalie decided to talk to himself in made-up voices on the radio and was never seen on ice again. The only ice he visits now floats in his drink.

20 MEN MUST STICK TO MANLY DRINKS

First of all, as you can imagine, I don't like being told what I can and cannot drink. Unless there is a section in the Bible I'm unaware of that is a follow-up to the Ten Commandments, let's say like the Book of Mixeronomy, I'm pretty sure I can drink whatever I want, when I want it, and with whom I want. There has always been an insinuation about what a man can drink, but that was mostly because of what was available at the time. Or, the ramifications of not following these rules wouldn't end in other men just rolling their eyes or calling you the proverbial "pussy"; you'd probably have the shit kicked out of you, or be shot in the head. Both really tough endings, all because you didn't drink a whiskey and decided to order a Planter's Punch in the "ol' saloon."

I think what I am talking about here is your ability to order the beverage, cocktail, or wine that suits the mood and the company. Would you in your wildest dreams order a giant cocktail that comes in a pineapple with a straw, filled with pink fruit juices, and loaded with four different kinds of liquors?

Not at home, but at a swim-up bar in Cancun surrounded by Hawaiian Tropic–style bikini chicks who strike up a conversation and bat their eyes, and who decide that ordering everyone giant pineapple drinks called "El Pinky Dinkies" is a great idea—trust me, you're in. Are you seriously going to order a Coors Light? You can, but it's another night of frustration for you, while that goof from France is with that Megan Fox look-alike, and you can hear her yelling from the beach, "These are the bestest drinks ever!" Well, I guess you can always buy those Mexican editions of *People* magazine from down at the concierge, Coors boy.

I'm not saying when you go to the hockey game, you want to be ordering a peach cooler in front of the boys, but what I am saying is if the choice of beer is wretched, finding an alternative, something you like, is completely acceptable. I went to a hurling match in Dublin with cousins Mark and Terry, my father-in-law, and my brother Dave. Brilliant it was! Croke Park, a hurling semi-final between Clare and Limerick, and the Guinness was being poured fresh right at the concession stand. I was in heaven! But to begin with, a quick pint of Magners Cider, to get me started before the onslaught of the "black stuff," which I thought was a good idea. The others looked at me, I felt a slight awkwardness, and then it was agreed, "Dat's a good f*%#ing idea," and then we all got one. Right mood, right choice, and then a whole bunch of Guinness followed by Jameson afterwards at the pub! Ireland is God's island. Maybe Bono is right: Maybe he is Jesus …

Brown liquor is a great liquor for a man: no question. Scotch is sophisticated; Irish whiskey is a great call anytime; bourbon makes me feel superhuman; rye built Canada (plus they drink it on *Mad Men*)—and they all make you look great while sitting at a bar, smoking a cigar, or enjoying the sorts of things grown-ups do. But sometimes, what you mix it with can also be a hard lesson. Remember: What is the mood and who is the company? I was dating a beautiful girl, who would later become a television anchor, and we went to visit her mother in a lovely, decorated upscale apartment. Her family was from old money. Her mom asked me what I would like to drink. I was a little nervous and blurted out my go-to drink. "A rye and ginger, please," I said, stumbling, like I was doing an impression of Bob Newhart. She said nothing, turned around, walked away into another room, and then said out loud, as she was mixing the drink, "My father once told me, if you can't drink right, you shouldn't drink at all." Boom, I got nailed! Shot down because I broke one of my cardinal rules: Who is the company?

So drink what you want. You know what you like more than anybody else on the planet, but remember who you are with, as the fallout from a bad decision can be embarrassing. I'll never forget ordering a Blue Lagoon at the Legion in North Bay. Bad call.

21 TRACK AND FIELD ISN'T IMPORTANT

A lot of people were wondering why Norway was cleaning up in the Nordic events at the Sochi games, while Sweden was not. I mean, Sweden is the bigger country and both the Swedes and the Norwegians like skiing, right? So where were the Swedes when they were handing out medals?

Part of the answer came on the last day of the Olympics, when Sweden played Canada for the gold medal in men's hockey. See where I am going with this? In Sweden, the elite athletes are attracted to hockey. In Norway, they're not. Which leaves a lot of talent for other things. Like cross-country skiing.

This brings us to Canada. Sure, minor-hockey registration is dropping, but that's largely because even the youngest kids are being groomed to be stars. The elite kids are still there. It's the kids who used to play just for fun who are doing other things. If you're a naturally gifted athlete in Canada, you're probably playing AAA hockey somewhere. Hockey absorbs a ton of talent here.

That's fine. Hey, if you want to play hockey, play hockey. I'm the last guy who is going to talk anyone out of playing some puck. But while we're going on about how much we love our favourite game, I'm going to make a pitch for our most underrated discipline: track and field.

For some reason in our culture, track and field is seen as little more than a day off in elementary school. Track Day, which is sometimes called Sports Day. Why do we let this idea of sports fade as our kids get older? And can you question the amount of fun they have on this special day? You just have to teach, watch your kids, or volunteer to see it. The problem is that it should never have been seen as a one-day sport.

Track and field is the most undervalued athletic sport in Canada. There should be more emphasis on the skills and training that it takes to participate in it so there can be better knowledge of what it actually is: the foundation of all sports. You show me great track and field skills at a young age and I'll show you a child who has the foundation to play numerous sports with a real head start in terms of understanding training.

So why is track and field so underappreciated as a sport? In Canada, that's easy: hockey. The way hockey was taught, coached, and practised up until we met the Soviets in 1972 was that it was a game with a skill set unto itself. There was no immediate connection between what was taught in hockey and what was done in other sports that weren't performed on ice. After all, how could any other sport propel advancement in hockey skills when none of the other sports were played with skates? Certainly not figure skating! That was for boys who weren't strong or tough enough for hockey. Boys who might be attracted by sequins.

Since the '72 Summit Series, with numerous international hockey tournaments, challenges, World Cups, and Olympics, we as a hockey nation have learned from the Europeans and their understanding of total physical fitness. Soccer, core training, and circuit training have all been implemented into the regimen of what our kids have come to know as a part of hockey. But we still don't appreciate the skills and the fun that can be learned from track and field.

As a kid, I was a track athlete. I loved many events, but none as much as the triple jump. I remember some of my hockey buddies staring at me as hockey would end in the spring and I would immediately start doing "bounding drills" outside. "What the f*%& are you doing?!" Ironically, since the interchanging of ideas with our hockey-playing European friends, the drills I was doing are now commonplace in hockey training.

I also loved the 400-metre hurdles and long jump. They were excellent training for the body, good for hockey, great for the self-esteem, and in high school, an excellent way of meeting chicks. I believe this is called *win-win*. If I'm not mistaken, I still hold some records at my high school in track and field. I'm proud of them because they were only a part of what I did athletically as a student-athlete. I was first and foremost always seen in my part of southern Ontario as "the goalie." I never joined a track club or specialized in one event, as is the common practice in that sport. Sometimes, if you went to the provincial track and field championships, you would have to compete with eventual Olympians. But that was okay. I loved it, and I'm still proud of my personal bests: 400 metres—51.0 (flat); 400 hurdles—59.2; long jump—6.32 (metres); triple jump—13.32 (metres). Pull up a chair, and I'll tell you all about each one.

Look, I'm not trying to make anyone into a triple jumper, and I'm not making a case that we should "own the podium" at the Summer Olympics. *I'm saying track is fun.* I'm also saying Norwegians are fun, but that's another subject.

22 WE NEED TO PUNISH PEOPLE FOR WHAT THEY THINK

With the news that NBA commissioner Adam Silver had banned the "despicable" Donald Sterling "for life" from any relationship, business dealings, or participation of any kind with the league, the world rejoiced. Not just the sports world—pretty much anyone who doesn't have time for racism was happy to see this buffoonish mogul get what was coming to him.

On top of the lifetime ban, Silver issued a $2.5 million fine and said he will force Sterling to sell the Los Angeles Clippers. That's got to hurt, even for a billionaire. So this is a win for a North American society that has strived for equality for all peoples, and a victory against bigotry, racism, and discrimination. Yes? Maybe?

Sort of?

Well, it is undeniable that Donald Sterling already had a long and relatively well-known resumé that included discrimination. Sterling was sued for housing discrimination by nineteen plaintiffs in 2003, according to the Associated Press. In this case, he was accused of trying to drive blacks and Latinos out of buildings he owned. In November, Sterling was ordered to pay a massive settlement. Terms were not disclosed, but the presiding judge said it was "one of the largest" settlements ever in this sort of case. Sterling also had to pay $5 million just for the plaintiffs' attorney fees.

So my first question is this: Was Sterling's girlfriend's secret recording really the first hint that this guy is a raging racist? Was the NBA really all that shocked by the news?

Look, the NBA has *always* known what Donald Sterling was about. We might not have known, but the league had to. And as long as we didn't, maybe everything was okay. Let's put it this way: You have to admit it's a pretty weird fluke that this 80-year-old billionaire's conniving tramp of a girlfriend recorded over a hundred hours of private conversations—and then made them public. If not for this truly bizarre behaviour, it would be business as usual at the ol' OKKK Clipper Corral. Right? So let's be clear. The real problem here is not that Donald Sterling got caught. It's that the NBA had him as a member of its select group in the first place.

Is ridding the league of a morally bankrupt slumlord a good idea? Yes. Does it truly address racism in the NBA? Don't kid yourself.

And before everyone starts applauding the fact that Donald Sterling was exposed, be careful what you wish for. We live in a TMZ world where everybody has a camera/recording device/videophone. The same players who are repulsed by the comments made by a racially biased owner need to know that the same sword that cut the head off Sterling is just as sharp for them. Just as sharp for all of us. Would everything you say to your friends be so inoffensive that you'd be happy hearing it played back on CNN?

At the core of this issue is not just condemning those who are easy and obvious targets, and congratulating ourselves for not being as backwards as Donald Sterling. We need to ask, "What is a reasonable expectation of any owner, in any business, beyond being fiscally responsible and successful?" I believe the public dismantling of Sterling isn't progress—it's just a case of bad business, being made public by a sloppy and degenerating billionaire. Will we see an improvement in the quality of character in the NBA because of this? We won't know until the next entrepreneur purchases another losing team in a losing market—and takes their net worth from the equivalent of $12 million to $600 million, like Sterling did—but is also is a man of "fairness and high moral fibre."

Excuse me if I don't hold my breath.

23 *EVERYONE LIKES BASEBALL*

Well, it seems everyone in the world plays it. So it must follow that everyone likes it, right?

I think it's fair to say that along with soccer (a.k.a. football), baseball is one of the world's most popular sports. I'm not counting cricket here, as it is not considered a North American sport, and, to be honest, I don't know what the hell it is. I know they wear a lot of white. I think a game lasts for a week. The word *test* shows up in their sport, therefore, I'm out.

Of all the sports that we play in North America, baseball is the most different. For those who love team sports, games that have contact, sports with constant action (such as running or skating), baseball is the odd man out. It is indeed a pastime. There is a focus on the mental game between pitcher and batter. Although there are other teammates in the field of play, the isolation of the duel that goes on between the pitcher and batter separates it from almost any other sport. This, I believe, is where the constant spitting, chewing, and scratching come from: The guys are bored. And just look at the variety of materials used by the baseball player to occupy time: chaw, dip (Snuff, Copenhagen, Skoal, various Bandits), sunflower seeds, and gum. This is the only sport where people feel bad for the turf.

Now in fairness, baseball does not look the same everywhere in the world. Games in Latin America are a show unto themselves. A case in point: the World Baseball Classic. Team USA apparently had a "home game" in Miami against the Dominican Republic. The park was filled with Dominicans and other Latinos with drums, horns, and whistles, completely energizing the stadium like it was Mardi Gras in Rio. It was fantastic, and it completely brought the magic of how baseball is played and followed in one of the world's great baseball countries, the Dominican Republic. If that was a home game for the United States, then Tony Montana was from Idaho.

To me, the best part about baseball is the month of October. Baseball playoffs take on a completely different feel from those in the regular season. For one thing, after 162 games featuring three quarters of the teams being out of the playoff picture since June, you start looking for meaningful games. Not that I don't enjoy watching a Houston Astros and Chicago White Sox doubleheader, which is game number 111 and 112 of the season, but I need that time to take up new hobbies, like sniffing glue or burning ants with a magnifying glass. Every pitch in October counts, as does every hit and stolen base, and a miscalculation in any facet of the game is death. Baseball moments are also filled with a kind of tragedy that seemingly lives forever in our memories, or, even worse, in the memories of those players who committed them. Just ask Bill Buckner.

So is baseball liked by everybody? Well, those who like it, love it. And the baseball freaks, they are a breed unto themselves. Ever see the guy who scores the ballgame in the stands with a scorecard? What the hell is that? Does he get chicks with that kind of activity? Ever overhear baseball fanatics talk baseball stats? It's like two mathletes trying to out-nerd each other to the death. So if you like baseball, good for you, but do yourself a favour: The next time you want to blurt out a stat about Dennis Eckersley or Yasiel Puig in the office or on a blind date, keep it to yourself. You don't want to be known as "that guy." And if you turn people off with your baseball blather, you might be a step away from liking cricket. And you don't want that. You don't look good in white.

24 EXPANDED NFL PLAYOFFS IS A GOOD THING

You like football, right? Which means that you like *more* football even more.

Or do you?

No. The dilution of the game has already pushed the quality into a middle ground. This system rewards the mediocre. Sure, your favourite team has a better chance of making the playoffs, so fans are likely to endorse another round of playoffs for exactly that reason. And Roger Goodell knows it. But the only organizations truly rewarded in this case are the National Football League, with the lucrative television and advertising dollars that follow more games, and the sub-.500 football teams that would've never been considered for the playoffs otherwise.

Look, I'll be honest, I watch football of all kinds, including bowl games that only friends and family care about. If on December 11, East Arkansas State Institute of Podiatry plays Rhode Island College of Good Spelling, featured in the Ashley Madison Horn Bowl and seen on ESPN 5, "The Cinqo," I'm probably watching it. I have no expectations from these schools; therefore, I'm not going to be disappointed by weak play. It's just one more night of watching football. (And yes, there are some games even I won't bet on.)

But, therein lies the evil that is the monster of the game of football in the United States: You put gridiron on TV, viewers will come. In 1970, there were eleven bowl games, starting on December 12 and ending on the traditional January 2, with New Year's Day being the "big day." Oh and what a day it was! The names, we all knew the names: Peach, Rose, Cotton, Orange, Sugar, and Bluebonnet! Ahhh, the world made sense and I was in love with Laurie Partridge! Now, there are thirty-five (35) bowl games! What? Names like Belk Bowl, Beef O'Brady's, and Tax Slayer.com rain upon us like a tsunami of football sludge, ending on January 6. At some point, is there really any integrity left?

Now, the NFL is going to venture down the road of evil to feed the football-addicted masses and give them all they can watch. But shouldn't there be a higher standard from the league itself to ensure those that make it to the post-season are worthy of being there? Just getting into the playoffs should be an achievement. It should be hard to get there. After all, isn't it supposed to be the most competitive football league in the world?

It's one thing for small or mid-major football programs to cash in on newly created bowl games to achieve status, some monetary reward, and televised recognition in hopes of building up their programs and possibly increasing awareness for recruitment. But how can it be said that, aside from the obvious financial benefit for the NFL and its owners, allowing into the playoffs a 7–9 Tennessee Titans or 8–8 Cleveland Browns team does anything but lessen the credibility of the league itself? If you want to brag about the quality of your league, then you cannot water down the process, like a barkeep who slides occasional drops of lesser liquor into an open bottle of Louis the XIII Cognac.

I love football of any kind, which most of you know. And I will bet on almost any game. But I also recognize when I'm being taken advantage of, and having a Jacksonville Jaguars versus Arizona Cardinals play-in game is exactly that. I know the NFL is going to do it and they're a business whose product is insanely popular, but I just saw Roger Goodell put a few drops of High River Rye into the cognac bottle. We are not amused.

25 *KNOWING WINE ISN'T IMPORTANT*

Wine is for pussies and guys in berets, right?

Wrong.

Remember the scene in *A Bronx Tale* where the beer-drinking bikers try to take over the wine-drinking wise guys' bar? If there is anything we can learn from the movie, it's that sometimes it's good to be a wine drinker.

I'm not talking about being a wine snob. You don't need a turtleneck for this. No one likes a wine snob, not even wine drinkers. So don't worry.

But today, lacking a fundamental understanding of wine doesn't do you any favours. The fact is, if you're between the ages of 30 and 55, you're part of a generation in Canada that started drinking and understanding wine to a level your parents never did. Most Canadians can now be given a wine list and have a pretty good understanding of the labels and the vintages listed.

The basic understanding that you need about wine is the relationship it has with food and cooking. Why is this important?

(See chapter 12, "A Guy Has to Be the Total Package to Get Girls.") Always remember that wine is food, and your ability to talk about it and implement wine choices at home or at a restaurant opens up social channels as well. Want to be a better cook? Learn about wine pairings. Of course, there is the challenge of trying to pronounce your new-found loves! OK, Amarone, one of my favourite and go-to wines from Italy, is pronounced ah-mah-RON-eh. I know you'll feel like a goof when first pronouncing this stuff, but style points count, especially on a date when the server repeats your order and says it correctly. Trust me, your date isn't saying anything, but she is thinking she is on a date with Matt Dillon from *There's Something About Mary*.

As we discuss in the chapter about golf and business, stoking your wine knowledge helps to make you look capable in business situations. Depending on your vocation, the *power lunch* or *business dinner* may become a part of your world. Making the right choice on the spur of the moment in front of your boss, and possibly clients, is a surefire game-winner all around. On the other hand, if you happen to ask a server or a sommelier in a finer establishment if Little Penguin is in stock ... there goes the promotion.

Hey, the jerk store just called, and they ran out of you!

Now keep in mind, you may enjoy imbibing these wines at home, and I reiterate there is nothing worse than a wine snob, so guzzle plonk all you like. Seriously, I am not going to judge. But you have to up your game in public, especially in a business setting. I like barbecue corn chips, but I wouldn't order them in public with my foie gras.

Knowing wine also helps you accomplish something beyond setting the mood and accentuating a great meal (and just tasting great wine—let's not forget that drinking it is the best part): It educates you about cultures you never would have discovered otherwise, on a level much deeper than you could have anticipated. If you have travelled before, you may now want to visit wineries and vineyards instead of the usual tourist attractions and landmarks. You will have a curiosity about the people and towns who make the wines you enjoy so much. The generations it took to perfect that bottle of wine you purchase in a liquor store down the street now sits majestically in front of you, complete with rolling hills, stone farmhouses, and family members who have worked that land for perhaps three hundred years.

So the next time you walk into a liquor store and an employee asks if you need help, don't give them the ol' "no thanks, I'm good." Ask them what goes well with the dish you're cooking. Tell them what you normally like and ask if they have a similar selection. Mention the grape from the country of origin that you constantly buy from and find out if it is available from another country. Canada is becoming a more savvy wine country and you do not want to be left behind. Oh, and when the liquor store employee asks you what you're looking for, try to refrain from answering, "What will get me laid?" It may be honest, but not appropriate. (By the way, it's Prosecco.)

26 *GAMBLING IS EVIL*

You never really see parents encouraging their kids to apply themselves a little more to their gambling. The Boy Scouts don't give out badges for beating the spread. And most of us have no fond memories of sitting on grandpa's knee, learning the finer points of making a bet.

And I think that's a shame.

So let's try to answer the question of whether there is anything morally questionable about gambling with some sensitivity, due diligence, and maturity, respecting the mores of certain groups, with an open-mindedness and a sense of decorum. Ready?

Gambling f*%#ing ROCKS!!!

I'm getting excited just thinking about it. Oh baby! *Action*, *skin*, *parlays*, and *chalk* are all sexy words—pillow talk for the gambler. But in all honesty, you have to define what kind of gambler you are. For most of us, a small wager just adds to the entertainment of the game. You could use the term *recreational gambling* as opposed to the serious bettor who will lay ten "nickels" on a single game—those guys are the pros, sharps, and individuals who make their living off of the gaming industry. And if you ask me, neither of those is evil.

The evil part is the inability to draw a line when the recreation starts to cause the financial or emotional problems we all hear about. That's addiction, not gambling. You know, people living in cars, losing homes, wearing Depends, and losing everything they ever had for the rush of the "big score." For me, I would think that at the moment you become convinced you should wear undergarments that facilitate soiling yourself in order to allow you a few more minutes playing the "Price Is Right" slot machine, maybe this has gone too far. (And yes, people do this.) "Hey, why aren't the ladies coming near me? Is it because I'm pooing my pants while I've just finished my eighth hour of mastering 'Lord of the Rings' and I have no money for socks or soap?" Some women are so picky.

For recreational gamblers, the rush comes from even the smallest amount of monetary gain, because it verifies that you have this incredible knowledge that (quite frankly) no one else has. This is why the office pool winner always has that glow of superiority and advice for those who aren't great and wise. Unwanted advice, such as, "You know, when I was analyzing the Tennessee–Buffalo game, I thought to myself, 'C'mon, Danny, you know that Buffalo doesn't play well on a Thursday night on natural turf when the date of the game is an odd number.'" Geez, Danny, your stats and research are amazing. I hope you don't get the Ebola virus and start bleeding through your eyes.

Gambling also brings us into locales we normally would not have visited in the first place, like Las Vegas. Why would I think in my lifetime that I could be sitting poolside in some decadent cabana, surrounded by little hard bodies, while designated staff bring me drinks and food as I prepare for a night of big-time shows, small-time wagering, and extra drinking followed by a decadent meal at 2:00 A.M., only to fall back on a king-size bed in a luxury suite overlooking the strip? I'm not Elvis or Sinatra, but I feel like it tonight, and for four days a year, the fantasy seems real and it's why we all go back. Thank you, Vegas, and, hey, tell Sammy that next time dinner at B&B Ristorante is on me!

So, thank you, gambling—you are our friend. Sometimes you hurt us, but you're always there waiting, urging us to try again, like the sexy bad girlfriend we've all had. And just like with her, we keep going back for more, because there's always that chance of a win this time. Oh, to hell with it! On with the Depends: Look out "Wizard of Oz" game, here comes Daddy and he's a-pooin' his pants!

27 HARD-ASSES ARE NEVER NEEDED ON A TEAM

Everybody likes the captain with the gleaming smile, the quarterback with the *GQ* haircut and the boy-next-door wholesomeness. And we all love to watch pure talent. From beer league to the pros, it would be nice if you could win with a bunch of great guys who happen to be gifted athletes.

Too bad that's not how it works. If you want to put together a great team, you're going to need a hard-ass on the roster. Let me give you an example. One of the greatest dynasties in all team sports, the New Zealand All Blacks of the late '80s, was head and shoulders above everyone else. They were good before that, of course. And they have been among the elite of the rugby world ever since. If the average sports fan knows one thing about rugby, it's that the All Blacks are a seemingly endless dynasty. But for those few years, they weren't just good; they were invincible. Literally. From 1987 to 1990, they went 47–0.

The captain for every one of those games was a guy about as hard-ass as they come. Buck Shelford. In the last game New

Zealand would lose for years, he first had several teeth kicked out, but he played on. Then he had a scrap. Then came the moment that may give you nightmares once you've read about it. While he was lying at the bottom of a pile of bodies, a French player stamped on his groin. With his cleats. Which sounds painful, right? But he didn't just have bruised nards. His sack had been ripped right open. Now, most guys would call it a game at that point. Not Shelford. Right there on the bench he had the package sewn up (without anaesthetic, of course). Then, game on.

Think that didn't inspire his teammates? Shelford was finally literally knocked out of that game with a concussion. But in the next game, he was the captain. And the All Blacks didn't lose again until Shelford lost his captaincy years later.

You have to recognize that on a team there are all kinds of personalities. The hard-ass is a guarantee when playing sports, or really in any facet of life where competition is involved. But let's define exactly what a hard-ass is: It's an individual who refuses to lie down without a fight, is relentless in the pursuit of winning at all costs, and is unwilling to compromise team goals once they're set. These goals are extremely difficult to achieve and the hard-ass tends to take ownership of them. The hard-ass personality is often not an easy one to work with, or to coach. Sometimes, a trait of a hard-ass is an unwillingness to listen to reason. These people feel that in heeding reasonable advice, they would be breaking their own *code*, a sign of personal weakness, even if the advice given is quite sound.

Some of the greatest championship teams had a core of hard-ass players who formed the persona of the team, and, in turn, the team reflected that personality. The Pittsburgh Steelers of the 1970s, the Broad Street Bullies teams iced by the Philadelphia Flyers, and the 1989 Detroit Pistons would easily fall into this category of hard-assedness, but it should be pointed out that this personality type is defined by more than just physical toughness. Maurice "Rocket" Richard, Gordie Howe, Bobby Clarke ... the list of Hall of Famers you wouldn't want to mess with could go on for a while.

Now keep in mind that we have talked about the hard-assed personalities as they appear on a roster. What if your coach is the one who's hard-assed? A lot of the viewing public has a general consensus on what a hard-assed coach looks like: Mike Ditka, Fred Shero, Woody Hayes, or Bobby Knight. (All, by the way, have won championships.) It is also fair to say that most people have a low tolerance for that kind of coaching, and in fact may believe that style has gone the way of the dodo bird. Although I agree that the fire-and-brimstone style of coaching is probably outdated, not all hard-assed coaches are necessarily bombastic. But those who have that toughness in their method can be successful for a very long time. I'm sure playing for Scotty Bowman was never a picnic, and you may have to go a long way to find a more difficult coach to play for, but you were almost guaranteed one thing: winning. Ken Hitchcock will push you to extremes, but his excellent track record speaks for itself.

Now, we're talking about winners here. A hard-ass on a losing team may just be called a jerk. The guy who will stop at nothing to win is probably not easy to get along with, and he's probably the first guy to cross the line. But if you want to win, a hard-ass is probably in the dressing room somewhere.

28 INSTANT REPLAY IS OVERUSED

You know what my favourite part of the game is? Staring at the ice (or the field, or the court) while someone, somewhere, decides whether or not the score I just witnessed is going to count.

I certainly know why some people would feel that replay is overused, but the reality is that reviewing a play in sports is now what people expect. There used to be a notion in football that when officials reviewed a play by video, the process would take too long and the flow of the game would be greatly hindered. They weren't wrong: It was clumsy and time-consuming. But perhaps the biggest problem was we had never sat through video review before, so, because we weren't used to it, we were wondering whether this really was the right way to correct a perceived mistake. Were the officials so wrong (from time to time) that we needed this process to make the game better?

Well, actually, yes. Yes they were, and yes they are.

It's Sunday and you're watching a football game. A pass is

thrown and called complete on the field, but you as spectator, whether cheering for or against the attempted catch, are unsure. Tell me your first reaction. Of course, you immediately expect a ruling on the play. It's second nature. An expected procedure to make sure they get the *call right*. And a funny thing has happened: No one is overly upset about the time it takes any more. The emphasis now is always about getting the call right. But this example is about football. Are we as fans still good with the reviewing process in other sports?

Now I should state that there are times when I find the whole process challenging as a fan. In hockey, never in my lifetime did I expect to see the fifty-seven angled cameras around, on top, and in the net. A camera *in* the net? Being a former goalie, I wonder if they can see everything. I don't want them to see everything, like when, during a period, I would scrape the ice in the crease for a long time and pack the snow close to the inside of the posts, just in case. I still remember in one particular game when a ref came by my net, kind of smiling, kicking the frozen mini walls down with his skate and then saying in as serious a voice as he could muster, "No snow forts." How would the discussion on that have gone during the second intermission on TSN's hockey panel?

JAMES DUTHIE: What do we make of the ref knocking down Richards's snow walls?

BOB MCKENZIE: He's been doing it his whole career even going back to midget, all the way through to the Peterborough Petes. In fact, during his play in the world juniors, the Russians always complained about his *ice fortress*. This is no surprise to me.

JAMIE MCLENNAN: I don't see anything wrong with it. I used planks of wood with nails ...

JEFF O'NEILL: Get off his back! Do they know how much this guy drinks? If you can play like that after downing three pitchers of sangria before the game, I think this guy is on his way to the Hall of Fame.

AARON EARD: He sickens me. I'd like to punch him in the face.

Oh, and in 2014, we were introduced to maybe the biggest argument for video replay invading all aspects of sport: video review in baseball. That's right, baseball! The pastime of peanuts, popcorn, and Cracker Jacks—a sport so slow at times that you could shave during a game and not miss much—now ventures into the world of electronic correction. Babe Ruth would be rolling in his grave, which means he'd crush the bones of the three hookers that are buried with him, not to mention the smushing of the Cuban cigars that were concealed inside the enormous suit in which he was buried.

Replay is here because the vast majority in this world, craving ultimate perfection in everything we do, want it here—in fact, demand it here. And if you don't believe me, I'll come to your house and start smashing things! Oops ... sorry, I didn't mean to say that! Let's forget that ... oh no, too late: You just threw the challenge flag and they're going upstairs for "further review." I'm screwed. Damn video replay.

29 YOU CAN COUNT ON WASHROOM ETIQUETTE AT SPORTING EVENTS

Etiquette in men's rooms at stadiums? Ha! Good luck with that. It is its own untamed wild kingdom where only the strong survive! A dog-eat-dog existence, or in this case, we should say a dog-pee-dog existence. It's not an easy feeling finding yourself in "that line," say during halftime at a football game. Have you ever witnessed some of those faces? You can tell from their expressions that they may be "new fish" or first-timers. They can hear the sounds from inside the washroom, still seemingly miles away, but they can also hear the gen pop. What's all that yelling and laughing? What's going on in there? I've made a huge mistake, maybe I can hang on?! Sure, keep telling yourself that, fish: But they're always in there, always waiting, and they know you *have* to go some time ... HAHAHAHA! Sorry, too ominous? Well, let's try to break down the experience and the types of individual traits of those you see at the games and in the men's room.

Should you need to go, I find there are two distinct types of guys. First, there is "Johnny Pee Pants." This guy generally has to go even before the game begins. And even stranger, the experience doesn't seem to bother him. He's a regular attendee of the men's weekend, where you take a road trip from, let's say, Toronto to Detroit. This trip on average is four hours or less. Pee Pants will want to stop twice. Twice! How do you even work? Is there a urinal under your desk? Do you wear rubber pants? I don't get Johnny and I don't like him. Then there's the majority of sports "goers," and they are "Danny-Don't-Break-the-Seal." Most of us are "Dannys," and the visits are weighed against the ratio of drinking beer (and/or cocktails) to the amount of time you can hold off your first men's room visit, because as we know, for whatever scientific reason, once the "seal" is broken, you now venture into unknown territory. You have lost control of the ship. You are Sandra Bullock trying to control that bus and Dennis Hopper is your bladder. Trust me: You don't want this fight and "Danny" knows it.

When in the men's room lineup, the key is focus. Remember what you are there for; keep your eyes straight forward or down; no eye contact; no conversation with the other inmates; no looking over to see what the other guy is doing. And don't worry if there is no soap or paper towel—keep the line moving, always moving, and get the hell out of there alive! Oh sure, you'll hear sounds and conversations, but they're not for you. Go ahead, try looking in the direction that comment came from and you'll find a painted-faced, sweaty, frothy-mouthed diehard who has the whiff of twenty-seven Coors Lights on him, and invariably, he's a "close talker." Just keep walking. Don't look up: Wait your turn, pee, and move, always keep moving.

Oh, and the obvious other "fatal" faux pas: going number 2. No number 2. Never. There's no telling what evil lies behind those doors. I had a cousin, Kevin, who at a Ticats game decided that after devouring two "Hamilton Tube Steak au Pain" (hot dogs), he needed to "free the chocolate hostages," "launch a corn canoe," or "take the Browns to the Super Bowl." I begged him, pleaded with him, as the uncertainties of what lay behind that door were absolutely unimaginable! That was 1985. He never came back. I miss him to this day.

So venture to the men's room if you must, but remember, you're there for one reason and one reason only, for there are no rules. Don't be a Kevin.

30 YOU HAVE TO TAKE CARE OF YOURSELF

There was a time when I assumed that since I have always been more or less fit, I would always be more or less fit. As they say, people don't *really* change.

Not only is this incorrect, it's probably the hardest lesson most men learn, and at a place in their lives when they don't want to hear it. Ever thought to yourself how great it is to work out at the gym, the feeling you get from exercising, and then you realize you haven't really been on a regular basis in eight years? It sucks. The mirror doesn't lie and it's even worse to see your shape broadcast on national television. How could this happen? Did I not win all those trophies? Have I not been to the provincial championships in almost every sport that is played? Oh wait: That was high school and college. So the deal is, what you did twenty-five to thirty years ago won't necessarily carry over into your forties and fifties? And to think I've been consuming fine wines, imported liquors, and beautifully rolled cigars and that hasn't translated into me staying in tremendous physical shape?! Man, was I way off.

Now, when you say "gym" to a lot of guys that means you're talking about lifting weights. And why shouldn't it mean that? I'm not talking about that cardio crap that seems to be all the rage. Forget it! Men bench-press, squat, lift, and grunt; there's no spinning. Spinning is what happens in a washing machine or to those who can't handle their booze and I'll have no part of either. As an aside, I've never been around anyone who has ever said, "My head is spinning." I've seen it only in the movies, and to be honest, those are the characters that usually get a chainsaw ripped right through their midsection by a man wearing overalls and a Tony Esposito mask. I guess all that work on your abs and core aren't really any match for a psychopath with a McCulloch.

The reality is that cardio and diet start to play an evil role in middle age, and the truth is that it's more about your personal health than trying to get on the cover of *Ripped Magazine*. It is a fact for the aging male. I have met some guys who do have it right, and they are very honest about maintaining certain elements of their lifestyle, while recognizing the sacrifice it takes to do it. "I run marathons," one guy tells me, as we both scarf down red wine at a Christmas party. "Why?" I enquire. Slurp, slurp. He says, "So I can continue drinking wine." Guzzle, guzzle. "Good point," I reply. Gulp, gulp.

Do I have to give up my Gordon Ramsay–inspired sauces in order to return to a physique I recognize? Well, maybe I don't have to give them up, but I certainly need to try to achieve a balanced diet *with* continued and consistent exercise—this must be the goal in order to achieve a happy and healthy life. (And by "happy," I mean, "Daddy like drinky.")

So back I go to the treadmill and the elliptical, along with the weights. As I was told by one of my favourite people in Calgary, Stu Laird, "Every day is a bench day." (He'll hate that I put his name to this.) Wish me luck, as the annoyance of running, especially with the pin I now have in my right knee, will drive me crazy. And yet I can see it all now: new svelte pant sizes; hipster tight suits at black-tie affairs; singing solos at trendy nightclubs; and as I croon romantic ballads, women like Beverley Mahood swoon and say things like, "Oh, I do declare that Mike Richards and his tight pants are entirely too much for one woman to bear!" Yes! I can see it all now, but it does seem like a lot of work. I will miss the beautiful and heavy-creamed sauces, the imported cheeses, and the artisanal breads. I wonder how much lipo costs? Yeah, liposuction! I could have it all: the pants, the singing, Beverley Mahood, and the cheeses! "Hook me up, Doctor Fatty. Turn the machine on high and get me a double rye and ginger with a side of bacon-wrapped scallops!"

31 PLAYERS ON A PROFESSIONAL TEAM SHOULD ALL BE TREATED THE SAME

Maybe there was a time when this was a common practice and philosophy. And possibly understandable, considering professional sports at the outset was just one way for individuals to put groceries on the table. It was a job, slightly unconventional, but not viewed as the best way to make a living. Hero worship was still pretty much a "college" entity. Professional leagues were considered a fledgling proposition at best in the early days and, therefore, those who played in them were treated pretty much like anybody else who had a "normal" job. You weren't special, privileged, or necessarily well paid: If you wanted the job, you did what you were told. This, of course, during a time when the phrase, "What's all the hubbub, bub?" was a question. Today, it's a rap song.

In modern professional sports, the head coach isn't just a guy in a suit who puts the fear of God in his players. I'm not saying that there isn't discipline—far from it. Not only do I believe it is necessary, but I also believe the players crave it. There has to be a sense of order in sport and that ultimately must be laid down by the coach. But the idea that discipline is maintained purely by yelling and threats is a fiction. The coaches who have reputations as taskmasters are becoming fewer and fewer, if not extinct. If the delivery of the message comes only with an "iron fist," I can almost assuredly tell you the second part of the sentence also contains the phrase "shelf life."

The modern-day coach is a bit of a Renaissance man. Mixing a stern message and methodology with a sensitivity about how to reach a modern-day athlete is a subtle balancing act that can achieve significant results. In hockey, bench bosses like Danny Bylsma and Paul MacLean represent the new tact in coaching, a balance of smarts and psychology. Even older coaches, who by definition may not outwardly appear to be this way, have adapted. You can make an argument for the excellent job Claude Julien has done in Boston.

NFL coaches by definition, if not by appearance, were the classic example of "I yell, you jump!" Long overcoats, fedoras rolled up, playbooks in hand, and, in the day, smoking, was an overall look that said, "Don't ask, just do!" Now don't get me wrong, it's not like I'm saying the current group of NFL coaches show up to practice with hot chocolate and Cinnabon, but the approach has evolved. No longer do coaches wear suits and coats on the sidelines—they are now more like one of the team, instead of someone who is visibly different or a step up from the players (think of the late, great Tom Landry). The hoodie-inspired coaches, the track suit, the visor, and the Under Armour generation now inhabit the sidelines. The Harbaughs, Pete Carroll, Mike Tomlin, and Sean Payton are all examples of modern-day coaches. Who is the top hoodie coach? Bill Belichick is in his own category. When contemplating the field boss whose first choice of sideline clothing would always be the hoodie, would you pick Belichick? No way. And you could argue that he still might be one of the only remaining coaches in any sport who could be spouting, "My way or the highway." But that's what winning Super Bowls does for you.

Okay, are you ready for the recipe? Here we go ... "Coaches, to reach the younger player, appeal to his sense of where he came from. For the star player, reinforce his ability to not only lead by example but also to inspire others who will only improve their play because of it. Treat the media fairly and develop a working relationship, because there will come a time when you may need their help in return." (Woody Hayes just read this and died again.)

32 PRO ATHLETES SHOULD KNOW WHEN TO RETIRE

God, don't you just hate watching old players dithering over retirement, spending the off-season "talking to their families" (as if that's a newsworthy item: "Player Talks to Family"), "seeing how they feel," considering their options—and then showing up to play another season (training camp optional).

I mean, look at these old guys, selfishly pursuing their own goals (like winning a Stanley Cup, or another Stanley Cup, or making millions of dollars). As a sports fan, I just hate seeing oldsters like Teemu Selanne showing up year after year, just so—wait, never mind. Selanne's awesome.

Then again, if you get to spend the summer deciding whether you really want to make millions of dollars playing a game you love, chances are you're awesome, too. Hi, Jaromir.

The fact is, the number of guys who get to play pro sports is tiny. As a percentage of the people who want to play pro sports, it's something like 0.00005 percent. And the number of guys who play pro sports and *also* get to leave on their own terms is much,

much smaller. The vast majority of the world's best athletes get shoved out the door the moment their bosses find a better, cheaper option. Or they suffer a career-ending injury. Or they're just forgotten. Maybe they get sent to the minors and never get called back. Maybe they're playing in Europe. Don't say this isn't true unless you can tell me Lonny Bohonos's stats from his last season in the German Elite League.

But a very rare group of guys goes out on their own terms. Like Selanne, Jagr, and Nick Lidstrom. (And, less appealingly, like Mats Sundin.) The ultimate swan song, though, was Gretzky's. It was a year-long retirement party that also happened to be his worst-ever season. He scored only 62 points that year, so he was clearly washed up. Because 62 points today would merely make you a multi-millionaire superstar. Yes, when Wayne sank to the level of superstar, he knew it was time to hang 'em up.

The question is, though, should anyone quit the moment they're not the very best on the planet? Where does that leave the guys who never were the best on the planet? We assume as fans that the glorious way to end a career is "when you're on top." It's a great theory and makes for a tremendous storyline, especially if it's a TV movie. Real life is never easy, especially when you have to give up what has been your main existence since childhood and has allowed you to live a life of privilege. But for most athletes, the privilege is not just monetary, which for the most part is the aspect the majority of the public will focus on.

The idea that everyone should retire the way Gretzky did is like saying that everyone should score 200 points in a season. It's not just implausible, it completely misinterprets what athletes are all about.

They're about sports, in case you're wondering. Yes, they're about the money. People will always see the money. The moment there was disclosure in professional sports, the general public became privy to what their favourite players made. And I doubt athletes hate getting paid. But that's not what drives them. The privilege that most players embrace is the fact that the game that they have played since childhood has allowed them an existence of male bonding, competitive gamesmanship, and the ability to travel with their "mates," without the mundane reality of normal day-to-day life. Their "play" is their "work."

Now don't get me wrong. This life is not given to any of them. The sacrifices they have made to get there most people don't comprehend. The amount of work pro athletes put in to get into the big leagues and stay there is insane. It's a lifetime of focusing on one thing, being away from your family for it, getting injured for it, thinking about it when you're rehabbing, and thinking about it when you're hitting the gym in the off-season. So, do you think it's easy to give up on something you've given everything to achieve in order to beat the odds?

(Okay, maybe some guys are thinking about the money: the ones who burned through every cent they ever made and more. Reckless spending is a part of some of the most shocking reports we have on pro athletes, and the general public has no sympathy for the likes of Lenny Dykstra, Terrell Owens, Allen Iverson, or Lawrence Taylor. Travis Henry, a former running back, has eleven children by ten "baby mamas." It boggles the mind how they even have the time to be that irresponsible.)

For these players, the game is everything. Here's what retirement looks like to them. The locker room, which has been your sanctuary: gone. Male shenanigans among teammates: gone. Chartered flights, first-class hotels, adoring fans: gone. But maybe the hardest thing to give up is the possibility of accomplishment. The work that went into winning a conference, a division, or a championship is a part of your soul that is irreplaceable. Moving on from that emotional attachment would be like severing a limb. Now, imagine having a job in which a good day of work can result in tens of thousands of people cheering their minds out, and in the spring, if you have sixteen good days at work, you get to realize a childhood dream. Might be hard to give up a job like that.

So the next time you catcall an older player for lingering in the pros, think on this: Would you give up the travel, the excitement of the game, the money, and the screaming fans? Could you easily wave to the standing crowd one last time while saying goodbye to your teammates? I know I'd keep playing until a giant, Pythonesque cartoon foot squashed me at centre field.

33 PROTESTS AND PICKETING ARE EFFECTIVE WAYS TO VOICE YOUR OPINION

Everyone has the right to an opinion. Luckily, I am here to provide you with mine.

In my opinion, protests are a waste of time.

I get that everyone has a right to free speech. Here's the thing, though. This right is made possible by our laws. If you want to question the laws, that's fine, I guess, but then I get to question your right to yap about what the rest of us are doing.

Just like in business, if you want to accomplish something, you have to ask yourself, "What is the endgame?" If you are fighting for some type of cause, what is the best way to sway public opinion? After all, as protesters are fond of pointing out, we live in a democracy. And in a democracy, it is the public who elect the men and women who eventually become the decision makers. So, are protesters accusing us of being bad voters? Uh, okay, I guess. But if they are trying to get us onside, how does stopping the public while they are trying to go to work help further their cause? "It brings awareness," always seems to be the answer. Really, you mean interrupting my commute makes me more aware? Your decision to grow dreadlocks makes *me* more aware? Gosh. Thanks.

Poor hygiene, angry placards, tired slogans ... these don't bring "awareness," I am sorry to say. What they generate is something called *anger*. Especially when waved in the face of people on their way to work to provide for their families. So you just pissed off the person you're trying to win over. Well played.

Here's the thing. If I don't want to stand beside you in the lineup at Tim's, I'm probably not taking your political advice. Would dressing decently *really* hurt your cause? Seriously. Try it. In fact, just think how welcome protesters might be if they dressed like cheerleaders in the 1950s and shouted out slogans through a megaphone while wholesome-looking ponytailed girls clapped their hands in unison and smiled? Just imagine, instead of yelling, "Down with the elitist banks! Capitalism rapes the people!" how about,

> Two, four, six, eight, what do we appreciate?
> Banks, Banks that treat us great,
> *Helping folks without the rape!*

I'm not going to do the protesters' work for them, though. So that's the last free cheer I write for them. And I will certainly not provide unintentional help to one of the most unwelcome varieties of protesters: those who sabotage rib fests. You know, those summertime events where friends and families come together to raise money for the town rink or the Rotary Club? Sounds awful, right? Well, better get out the placards. That's right, there is now a tradition of ruining rib fests. Why? Because these fests violate the rights of pigs. You may think I'm making this up. I wish.

Here's the thing. Even if you think that your ideas about pigs are more important than other people's families, do you really think that ruining those people's afternoons is going to bring them around to your way of thinking? Trust me, all you've made them want to do is punch you in the face.

Well, that and eat some more ribs.

34 SOCCER IS A BORING SPORT

For years, soccer and I had a complete disconnect, just like many other North Americans who couldn't get past some elements of the game. After several hours, the result is a scoreless draw? What? Was the stadium foggy? Did the players know the rules? Were there boards across the net? And what's with the rolling? Always with the rolling. You can't use your hands? Why? You have them: Maybe the games wouldn't be 0–0 if the players could throw the ball into the net.

So, is soccer a boring sport? The seemingly endless games, the pathetic scores, the scarves—and the singing? (Well, singing and fighting with broken bottles.) I have to admit, no. No, it's not. These days, I watch soccer that's played in nearly every part of the world. So now I feel I have to explain myself.

As it turns out, gambling explains a lot. As a young man sometimes does, I started gambling to while away the hours. At first, it involved my making bets on NFL football using Pro-Line. I won a couple of times, but I just didn't like certain matchups on some weekends and started to search for other sports to wager on. What was this English Premier League? Oh right, Liverpool and all that. Do people bet on this? I decided to take a chance and started to read and watch English football. Who is this Chelsea? Home of the buns? Arsenal? That name seems a tad insulting. So I bet on the EPL and kept watching and reading overseas blogs and columns. Then an epiphany! Maybe soccer games are being played elsewhere in the world and I could bet on them, too! What about Italy? Yeah, Italy! I have Italian friends and I've seen pictures of swarthy-looking men all dressed in blue with deep-set eyes like they were either going to make you the best cannelloni you ever had or kill someone. So, enter a lot of Serie A watching and yet more reading.

Then a funny thing occurred: I kept watching the games even when I wasn't betting on them. I watched the EPL, Serie A, Mexican football, Bundesliga, and then all the different cups, including UEFA Champions League, and, of course, the World Cup. I started to understand the culture, and how the culture influenced the style of football played.

And yeah, that's right, I now call it football.

I'll also say this, and this is true of any sport: You can't like a sport until you understand its rules and strategies. (Now this may not apply to cricket. I'm not getting the white pants. Only Robert Redford can wear white pants and get away with it.) Crosses, corners, set pieces, "flick-ons," and bicycle kicks are all now a part of my vernacular. And almost like playing catch-up with our compatriots from across the pond, another element of following football creeps into my consciousness: anger and resentment toward certain teams and countries. Hello, Thierry Henry and you cheatin' French bastards! (Sorry, but even though years have gone by, my Irish temper can never get over that Henry hand ball and the ensuing World Cup qualifier catastrophe! Feck off, you French eejits!)

So that is the truth. I like soccer ... ahem ... football. Now, the flopping and diving still gets on my nerves, and the feigning of injuries, with some players making like they have just been hit by one of Lee Harvey Oswald's bullets, makes me sick. Act like a man and play the game. But, as mentioned before, there are some cultures where trying to draw a card or penalty by embellishing a perceived illegal act is bred right into how kids are taught the game. But all that aside, go to a pub, sit with the boys, enjoy a pint, and learn the nuances of the game yourself. You'll find it doesn't take that long to be swept up into the emotion of a match. *Especially when the officials miss a hand ball by those lousy French cheatin' bastards and allow the people of Jesus to be victimized just like Cromwell was attacking the island once more with the evil imperialists from England!!* (Geez, I really need to let this go.)

35 WE NEED TO TALK TO EACH OTHER ON THE PHONE

Ever hear your BlackBerry, iPhone, or Benjamin Franklin–era cell phone ring, indicating an actual phone call and think, "Are you serious? What am I, the president?!"

If we can agree that society and its inventions are reflections of what we believe to be necessary, then the advent of texting and communicating non-verbally is a step forward for our society. We never *need* to actually talk to *anyone* on the phone, unless, of course, it's life-threatening or a chance of a sexual encounter. Even with our closest of friends, wouldn't you say the ratio of texting to talking is about 20:1? And it's not an insult, it's just math. If you had a conversation for every text you sent or received, you'd be on the phone all day.

Of course, this all goes completely out the window if you have a relationship where the other person is "texting impaired." It's probably a generational condition, as those under age 25 have basically grown up without having to talk to each other. LOL, ROFL, T2UL, :-) Have we become a race of people who can't stand our own race? Yes, because there are a lot of people out there we really don't *need* to talk to. You think this is rude? You don't believe this argument to be true?

Let's go back into ancient history, like 1979, and remember the annoyance of the telemarketer. It was foreign to us when it started, because we had to get our heads around the fact that someone we didn't know was calling at dinnertime to ask us if we wanted to subscribe to a newspaper we already got. Then phone companies started phoning us about phones ... telling us they had a better phone plan on the phone we were currently using. Did you enjoy those conversations? Well, we fixed that! The dual-cassette answering machine, courtesy of Radio Shack! Why did we do it? Because we realized we didn't want to take time away from whatever important thing we were in the midst of doing, like having dinner, watching the game, gambling, drinking, or having sex.

With further advancement in the telecommunications world, we embraced the idea of voice mail. And with voice mail came call display, and with call display came the ultimate weapon: call blocking! "Heeeee shoots and scooooooresssss!!" So not only can we see who is calling, giving us the choice of whether they are worthy of gaining an audience with us, but we can also decide if their conversation is wanted at all. "Hey, Smith and Farkus Lawn Maintenance, you have phoned one too many times and have been deemed an irritant to this household. Judgment: call block! You have been barred for life! No calls for you!"

With the advent of cellular communication, we have really stepped up our ability to ignore. But is it really ignoring or is it just allowing us to make our own decisions on when a full conversation fits into our schedules? Ever get a phone call from a close friend that you actually answer and get this conversation?

"Hey, did you see Peyton last night?" "Yes I did." "Wasn't he awesome?" "Yeah, he was. I watched the game with you at your house." "I have him on my fantasy team!" "Yes, I was there at the draft." "But wasn't he awesome?!" "Yeah, that's great, but I'm just at the doctor. I kinda have to go; he's putting a glove on. And by the way, when did you turn into Chris Farley?"

So don't be so hard on the how-come-you-never-pick-up guy, because there is probably a reasonable excuse for the times when you call that you can never seem to connect. And that reason is you. Call block. Delete from contacts. ROFL. :-)

36 HEADING TO THE STRIP JOINT IS A BAD IDEA

Okay, okay, you know it had to be in this book somewhere and you found it! The chapter on "modern dance."

Ah, the ol' peeler palace, the ballet, or gentlemen's club is a world and a universe all its own, with a set of rules, language, and etiquette that must be learned and adhered to. (Those beefy guys by the door, the only ones not smiling in the place? One of their jobs is to make sure these traditions are strictly kept.) Men have been burning money in these places since Eve said to Adam, "Look at these." They should be great fun, a source for laughs, and the best place to see hot chicks pretending to like you as the DJ pumps out Cinderella's "Nobody's Fool." But there is a strange sense of right and wrong at the "rippers," and the potential for wrong looms large for those who aren't careful. But what could go so wrong at a strip joint?

Well, for Lonely Larry, "it is the best of times, it is the worst of times." If your entire social interaction with women involves paying them to talk and dance for you in three-and-a-half-minute intervals, while feigning interest in your conversations about the "inaccuracies" of the zombie existence in *The Walking Dead*, you may have to accept that you're dying alone. If a dialogue comes up in the workplace, and you spout off names like Mercedes, Jaguar, or Porsche and you're not talking about cars, your resumé on Lavalife is scoring just above the guy who says, "My favourite scent is Mommy." You do feel sorry for these guys, but they are adults and if that's how they want to spend their money, who's to say, given certain social shortcomings, that this isn't a viable choice for their personal entertainment.

From the worst, threadbare, back-alley strip joints to the upscale, dress-coded gentlemen's clubs, the most glaring and most common pitfall for most normal functioning males is money. Oh, the pain of the next day. "I spent what?!" The glazed-over horror of the scribbled-out Visa receipts, the vodka-soaked ATM records with the always-reasonable bank machine service charge, and then the realization that your wife can see all these things, and even perhaps already has, while you're still trying to figure out whether it's possible that you may have lost your shoes somehow last night. How do you lose *shoes*?

But at the heart of it, the strip joint provides a great and extremely shallow night of cheesy fantasy, over-the-top cheap perfume, male bonding, and, most importantly, a quick vacation from the real world. Ever thought to yourself during a personal "dance" that "this chick is really into me"? Yes, you have! Don't lie! And you know what: You should. It's why we go. Then Porsche whispers into your ear, "Normally, I don't dance for men who are prettier than me ..." Boom! Did she really say that? Of course she did, and she is BANG ON!

The bumping and the grinding, all to some of the greatest hair band hits of all time—can there be a more mentally enlightening evening ever? When Helen Bed is twisting over you, tan lines exposed, in blazing-pink high-heeled shoes that look more like stilts, and wearing those thin chains around her waist that you want to eat like a warm spaghetti string, even Stephen Hawking would be popping a tent in his sweatpants, while broadcasting from his little electronic voice box in that monotone vocalization, "Make it rain. Make it rain."

So enjoy it for what it is: The girls want to take your money and God bless 'em, because I'm gonna give it to them. It's a night when we all get to feel a little like a rock star—no deep interaction and no attachments. The wafting smell of Eau de Peele, the bright lights, the snuggling, the giggling, the drinking with your pretend girlfriend for a couple of hours—how can this be wrong? Well, I'm sure it all is, but isn't it great?! So the next time you enter one of these establishments, play along with the fantasy, have fun with it—and maybe you have a "name" and a story, too. *"My name is Brandon Steele. I'm a medical consultant for a company that specializes in an infant breathing apparatus. I was married, but my wife died in a parachuting accident in Monaco. I'm alone now, but I have my work and I always have the children. It's always about the children."*

(Go ahead and use this. My gift to you. If it doesn't get the required result, just imitate Victor Newman.)

37 SWIMMING IS ONE OF THE TRUEST OF SPORTS

The original contests of man were essentially fighting, running, and swimming: true tests of strength, stamina, and overall athletic abilities. Pure competition. No judges, no points for style (and no shootout to break a tie). Just head-to-head action to see who's got what it takes. When you look at all the goofball sports that have made it into modern-day culture, some less challenging than others, it's hard to put down swimming as not being a "true" sport. It's tough to argue against this one.

But here's the thing: I hate it. The sport has bathing caps. Bathing caps?! I'm not wearing a bathing cap! What are we waiting for—FDR to come by in a raccoon-skin coat and a ukulele so we can all sing "Has Anybody Seen My Girl?"

There is the strength aspect of swimming that is very impressive, and the hours of practice and sacrifice it takes to perform the sport is mind-boggling. But if they don't have the capability to butterfly, front crawl, and backstroke for all those hours ... they drown. So the sport is based on just not dying. "Hey, Jim, that kid in the 200-metre individual medley is really something!" "That's right, Tom, and so far he hasn't died." "Right you are, Jim. A lot of swimming and very little drowning."

And let's talk about the most glaring problem with the sport of swimming: the suits. No one ever needs to see that much of a human being you don't know. Ever. (Those of you who know my position on gentlemen's clubs will think I am contradicting myself. Not so—have you learned nothing? The crucial difference between strip clubs and swimming clubs is that booze is served at the former and not the latter.) Now, the Speedo look might be all the rage on the beaches in Bulgaria, but I don't need to see Hans and his magical banana hammock destroying my new Samsung 65-inch 1080p piece of technological art. And now I'm regretting going with the 3-D option.

And is it me, or are there just way too many swimming events? What's freestyle? Can you just do anything you want? "Hey, Jim, after making the turn, that kid has a real nice dog paddle going on there!" "That's right, Tom, and if you'll notice, Svend in lane 7 is completely propelling himself with flatulence." "Right you are, Jim. And, of course, Svend is swimming for his brother Bjorn, who drowned during the 200-kilometre medley. As Svend put it, 'Bjorn just didn't realize how much swimming was involved.'"

Have you seen the breast stroke? Do you laugh when you hear the announcers say this? I do, but I'm immature. The thing that gets me about any of the swimming events is that it just doesn't look fun, including the faces they make during the breast stroke, and shouldn't an event called the breast stroke bring a smile to your face? And swimming should be fun. Just look what you do at the cottage or in a backyard pool. They should incorporate some of those activities into the actual races, like trying to make it to the end of the pool while your friends whip a football at your head or maybe the pool version of beer pong, an event that is both entertaining and nutritious for the participants.

Basically, we get it, "swim people." What you do is physically impressive. We just don't need to see it. You really want us to like your event? Throw piranhas in the water, have snipers in towers overlooking the pool, make the girls kiss in the water before the race is over—just do something. I'd like to offer more advice but I'm giving away this "gold" for free. Besides, I'm already working on some good stuff for diving: The "Cheerleader Pit of Fire" is going to be a huge hit.

38 THE TEN-GAME PARLAY IS A WASTE

For the real gambler, I'm sure three to four games are as far as they would go. But who wants to be a real gambler? The one aspect of gambling that gets talked about the least is the entertainment factor. Is there a reason to watch West Carolina versus Elon? No, but if the Catamounts and the whatever-Elon-is-called is your eighth game on your ten-game parlay, well that game has intensity written all over it! Having action on something is good, but on ten? That's crazy! Yeah, crazy like a fox. (Okay, so that phrase probably doesn't apply there.)

I look at it this way: You pay a small wager, perhaps looking at three or sometimes four sports, and let lady luck guide you to your rightfully earned fortunes. Unfortunately, lady luck is a bit of a bitch, and usually takes a dump on game number 7, or 4; in fact, I'm historically a 7–3 guy on average. Seventy percent is pretty good, but in the parlay world, you were just another guy who didn't win, looking at the box scores with a sad desperation, realizing that indeed you were not smarter than everyone else.

So, just what could you possibly lay money on in a ten-game parlay that would have you think that winning such a feat was possible? Well, the delusional mind is a wonderful place, my friends, and when you have won in the past, it feeds the fire of invincibility. My largest Pro-Line win was $21,000 on six games. Betting that year, 2004, after money spent, cleared almost $30,000. I had not really been gambling long, so sage advice fell on deaf ears. "You bet too many games." "Really," I replied, "I couldn't hear you because I was counting all my millions." In fact, it was thousands, and considering I was always paying off bills, the reality was, I wasn't counting much at all—but I was winning *and* paying off some debt. Why, what a great man I had become. But it doesn't last forever, and the huge wins don't always come, but the process of picking the games has become something like a religious ritual, and the games come from everywhere.

Here's an example of what a prototypical "Mike Richards-Parlay-a-Palooza" looks like, keeping in mind that the sports will shift with the changing of the seasons. In the fall, the ticket is usually two CFL games, five or six NCAA games, one or two soccer matches (usually EPL or Serie A), and three NFL games. The parlays have also included baseball, over/unders, French/Spanish/German/Portuguese soccer, and Gaelic sports. What? What Gaelic sports? Well, you haven't lived until you slap money down on hurling or Gaelic football! (Hurling is my new favourite thing, and watching a big game at Dublin's Croke Park makes you that much closer to going to heaven. If you don't believe that to be true, then I don't give a feck, you culchie eejit!)

There is also the fact, and it is an important distinction, that I'm not gambling because I need the money. I'm not a handicapper, or considered one of the "sharps," but a guy who thinks that picking a cavalcade of games is fun and entertaining. In fact, while writing this on a Saturday morning, I started a twelve-game parlay on Friday night. Before noon kickoff for NCAA football, I have already won three games: a Friday night NCAA game taking Central Florida +14.5 (beating previously undefeated Louisville), Calgary Stampeders –6 in the CFL, and Swansea straight up to win in the EPL. All right, now only nine more games to go! But such is the life of the ten-gamer, and I'm okay with that because the roller coaster of emotions will be tempered with cocktails and creative swearing. "So, get thee to thy internet and wager away, for the riches could be yours!" Oh, and by the way, don't tell your wife. Wives wreck everything.

39 *DEFENCE IS FOR TEAMS WITHOUT TALENT*

If you don't believe defence wins championships, then you probably haven't won very many. It really doesn't matter what sport we're talking about here, stopping people is a must in order to hoist a trophy. I also think there is some misunderstanding about what playing defence means. The moment you hear anybody talk about a great defensive team, a lot of sports fans will think "boring." It's probably the difference between being a fan and understanding the game.

Most coaches want defensive accountability. Meaning, it's not just a single-minded thought that defence is the only thing you have, but rather a responsibility that, in turn, is the beginning of your offence. Run and gun is fun, but that style in most sports usually gets crushed by the weight of a team that defensively carries a "bigger gun." Don't believe me? You can see this being played out right now in NCAA football: offensive pace versus traditional game planning.

Now, as many know, I once lived in Eugene, Oregon, as a kid.

That was the best experience ever for an eighth grader who was sports crazy. I had season tickets for the Oregon Ducks. Seems exciting now, but the success of the program in 1976 wasn't exactly what you have seen with the current Ducks. That year they were 4–7. I believe their offensive line may have consisted of two of the cast members from *The Facts of Life*. Fast forward to Chip Kelly, and his super-charged and fast-paced offence. It's infectious. It's exciting. Seemingly half of NCAA schools have tried to mimic it in one form or another. But in the end, powerhouses from the SEC show up and break everybody's spines. What? Oh yeah ... trust me, it's tough to argue that the most successful and the toughest teams in the SEC, and in general, run traditional offences and the meanest defences around. Championships don't lie: And it starts with D-E-F-E-N-C-E.

Hockey fans love to watch a "track meet." Is there anything better than a fast team, filled with dipsy-doodling stars, and a 6–4 final score? Yes, there is, as a matter of fact. It's called a "Stanley Cup." There is no question the skill set of modern-day NHLers is phenomenal. Every guy on the roster can fly. Every guy with a composite stick has a cannon of a shot (I mean, when Brian McGrattan is beating goalies from centre, it's safe to say that most players in the league can shoot it.) The talent level on the Edmonton Oilers alone would be enough to fill an all-star roster.

But those who grow the beards and drink champagne from Lord Stanley's chalice aren't just good hockey players. They're beasts. The one thing teams like Chicago, Boston, and that championship Kings team from Los Angeles understand is this: make going into their barn a physical nightmare for the other team. Oh, they have goal scorers, and guys who can dance. Now, let's see how they would like to receive an invitation to go into the corner a half-step ahead of Zdeno Chara or to try to set up in the slot alongside Chris Pronger. And it's not just pure physical menace either. Look at Team Canada in Sochi. Yeah, they had truly shocking amounts of firepower on that team. But that's not how they won. They won by not letting the other teams have the puck.

I also think that the eye rolling that goes on with hockey fans when coaches preach defence is the lack of understanding on how the transition game works. This to me is where hockey and basketball are the same game. The quicker you get the puck or ball back by playing good and sometimes pressure defence, the sooner you start your fast break. How is that boring?

I loved those Steve Nash–led Maverick teams with Dirk! They would go on those scoring frenzies on a nightly basis, make the highlight reels on every Sports Centre broadcast, and light up the scoreboard with 130 points or more. Other teams could score around 110 points, but it just didn't matter because the Mavs would simply outscore you—until the playoffs. Then teams that could play defence would hoist the trophy in June and spray the plastic-covered locker room in Cristal.

And you can't talk defence without mentioning the Pittsburgh Steelers. Try to wrap your head around an NFL defence allowing an average of just over three points a game. Or allowing only two touchdowns in a nine-game span. Your offence doesn't exactly have to shoot the lights out if the other team can't score. It worked for the Steelers—four Super Bowls in six years.

We all love offence, but we like championships better.

40 *DRINKING IS UNACCEPTABLE AT SPORTING EVENTS*

Here's a little history lesson for you. Booze has been sold at sporting venues in Ontario since the '90s. That's right. Beer and sports seems like a tradition, but it's actually a fairly new thing. I mean, we had cell phones before we were allowed to drink at a Leafs game.

Seriously. Thanks, Queen Victoria. No booze? What would you do if you were a Jacksonville Jaguars season-ticket holder? Maybe the question is, "Why are you a Jacksonville Jaguars season-ticket holder?" The mix of alcohol and sport at a live venue was fought against long and hard in Canada, especially in Toronto, where the influence of the bluebloods ran deep and so did the conservative dogma. For a long time, selling "the devil's brew" at a stadium or arena was considered taboo, especially for those who wanted to keep the sanctity of the game pure, just like its citizens. Ha! That's ol' Hogtown for you—the elders always knew what was best for its inhabitants because the people certainly were incapable of making the "right" decisions for themselves.

I remember going to old Exhibition Stadium in the late 1970s and early '80s where the vendors would go up and down the stands barking, "Coca-Cola! Ginger Ale! Makes a nice mixer!" Hmmm, I thought, what's a "mixer"? I know coming from me that sentence is either filled with irony or foreshadowing. (I don't know the difference. "I'm not that strong a swimmer.") Every single patron had conceived of literally a hundred different ways to smuggle booze into an Argos game. They even had cops to frisk you, not in the current "rubber glove" post-9/11 kind of way, mind you, but you still had to put some thought into the covert operation. So, why the booze? Well, for one, because of the way the Argos played from time to time (no Grey Cup wins for the Boatmen between 1952 and 1983). In fact, I believe this was the era when the haunting chant "ARRRGOOOOOS!!!" came about, and guess what? It wasn't used in a positive light. In fact, the Argos chant was dripping in sarcasm, just like the people in the crowd who were dripping in rye and rum from the multitude of flasks that had been smuggled into the stadium.

Drinking in the stands was a reflection of what the people wanted. But what contraband boozing brought was an unwelcome rowdiness that permeated throughout the stands and mixed young families and women with the unwelcome football version of Foster Brooks. With the advent of permitted alcohol, the powers that be then had the foresight to put in family sections, separating two very obviously different factions. It also allowed ownership of the sale of alcohol via the concession stands. It's not perfect. There are still drunks. But those individuals who would allow themselves to get hammered at a public sporting event would also do it in a Shoppers Drug Mart if they allowed open rum-and-Cokes in aisle 5 between the toothbrushes and the condoms. I believe these people are known as dicks.

The only complaint I have about booze at a stadium, and so has pretty much every other sane sports fan, is the price. Do they know how much these drinks really cost everywhere else in the world? (Well, everywhere except Idaho, where fans launched a class-action lawsuit against Boise's AHL rink for overpricing beer. See? The system works.) Are they shipping this magical beer and alcohol from some foreign land I'm unaware of, thus the price of the drink is similar to that of a small car? Look, if this rye is being made by naked Swedish virgins on a remote Nordic island, I can sure appreciate that. But can't you just give me a shot of the Wiser's? I'll pay for a normally priced drink and with the savings I'll go to the Brass Rail and meet an Eastern European girl who is also naked but not a virgin.

A little self-control by everyone makes this whole argument a lot easier. Just relax, have a cold one, and enjoy the game, unless, of course, you're a Jaguars fan, but that's your fault and no amount of alcohol in the world is gonna drink them good.

41 YOU CAN WEAR ANY TOP TO ANY STADIUM

You live in a free country, right? So you should be able to wear whatever you want to a sports game. Seems reasonable.

Except it isn't.

Look, I know it should be acceptable to wear your team's top to support the squad on the road. And the experience should be fun—that's why we go to the games, right? For the most part, especially in Canada, it's not a problem. But I would be careful, depending on the city and which team's fan base you choose to challenge. Because some people *will* see it as a challenge and will come at you with some abuse.

And that's the thing. It's not the sweater that's the issue, or your right to wear it. It's the way others react to it. It may not be right, but you have to be smart.

I got an email once from a woman who took her young boys to a Flames game wearing Oilers sweaters. She was appalled by the abusive language they received from young men as they walked through the lobby, especially post-game. As much as this kind of incident sickens me, if you go to enough rivalry games, there will always be a faction of drunken losers who have no idea about decency or decorum. How you can drop bombs on anyone, particularly children, is beyond me. It is also my experience, however, that these kinds of games have a higher moron-to-normal-people ratio.

Now, did this woman do anything wrong dressing up her boys the way she did? That's not the point. It's not about right and wrong. Do you really think that, as fun as it should be, wearing a sweater that will attract those kinds of mental defectives is a good choice?

In other countries, wearing the jersey of an opposing team is essentially forbidden. There are many instances in soccer wherein a certain team or country's colours can be fatal. The hooligans or soccer firms, the radicals who follow a football club, almost for the sole purpose of fighting, are very serious business. In places like that, not only in the stadium but also around town, wearing your team's scarf is like wearing gang colours. And we know how that works. We all get that you have the right to dress as you choose, but if you wear a Glasgow Rangers shirt into a bar full of Glasgow Celtic supporters, I hope you're a fast runner.

In and around the NFL, you take your life into your hands when you wear a visiting team's jersey. Old Veterans Stadium in Philadelphia had a full-time judge, court, and holding cell in the bottom of the building just to process the fans who couldn't control themselves. Put on a Chargers top, go to an Oakland Raiders game, and try sitting by some giant who looks like he just stepped off the set of *Star Wars*. Try making it to the parking lot without being "shived." And if there is no imminent physical threat, the verbal abuse is some of the worst I have ever experienced.

Oddly, the one league that generally embraces fans' enthusiasm for out-of-town teams is the CFL. These amazing fans have created a friendly jabbing toward each other, like cousins who wrestle on the ground while sharing beers. The Grey Cup might be one of the only championships where fans everywhere will celebrate a great team. (Note to self: Canadians are all right.)

So wear your opposing top proudly, if you really want to. Just don't come crying to me because what you thought was a fun way to support your team on the road was interpreted by local fans as a challenge. And you might want to give thanks every once in a while that your team doesn't play any road games in Glasgow.

42 CASINOS ARE BAD

Wrong. And really wrong. Casinos aren't bad. Casinos are good ... unless you live in Toronto, where a new casino venture was voted down. And why wouldn't the council members vote it down with all the dangers that emanate from casinos: the Tommy guns blazing, guys named Lefty and Johnny Three Thumbs walking around with brass knuckles, Joe Pesci burying guys in the sand, and all the plaid pants with white belts—well enough is enough! Just what decade do some Toronto councillors think we live in? Not that a casino doesn't come with social and logistical challenges, but I thought citizens in this part of the world were allowed to decide for themselves.

I didn't see Las Vegas and the world of casinos until I was in my thirties. I never played cards. Even on the hockey buses. (I spent a considerable amount of time looking at *Penthouse* magazines, which explains a lot.) I saw the bright lights, the crazy sounds, and the excitement around the tables. People laughing and shrieking over the "magic" of the slot machines, just waiting for that perfect spin. Of course, I was unaware of the Depends-wearing people. This may be what the shrieking was about. But who cares?! It's the allure of adults having fun with no kids, no deep conversation, no "How was your day?" My God, for any man out there, can there be a worse way to start a conversation than with those words?

Strange thing, though: I never visited a brothel, I never saw anybody shooting Tommy guns, I didn't get caught up in a drug deal gone bad, and I didn't end up on an episode of *Cops*. Now I know the reality of casino life is that it comes with all those potential elements. But with good management and due diligence among the planning committees, why can't there be a positive result for the community? Well, the reason given is always the same: dissention among those in the decision-making process. Not that they have the answers, they just "don't want it."

Well, guess what? The real people do! That's right. Good people, the good card-playing people, those that know fine cigars and make the waitresses giggle with impressions. The good stay-up-all-night people who play roulette to the wee hours and still know how to choose wisely from an extensive wine list. And let's not forget who is making all of this happen behind the scenes: local people who are now in the workforce because of the enormous need in this very specific service industry.

Oh, and I almost forgot. Casinos smell good! You know what I mean: "casino-ish." Yeah, that's a thing. You're walking down one of the carpeted aisles, maybe glancing at those on the slots, making your way to a blackjack or poker table, and in your head you hear Sinatra singing a classic, or maybe Dino—or for some, maybe it's the big brass stabs from a Bond movie—and then you do it: big inhale! And what do you smell? "Casino!" Yeah, baby, you're so money!

But if none of this appeals to you, including the shows, the dancing, the fine dining, and the people-watching, I guess that's okay, too. There's always staying at home, with Monopoly or KerPlunk. Perhaps reading alone with a good book does the trick. Or maybe, just maybe, you're Amish and it's time to build a barn, churn some butter, or be afraid of chrome. All good choices, I suppose. Oh and by the way, "How was your day?"

43 IF IT QUALIFIES AS AN OLYMPIC SPORT, IT'S A GOOD SPORT

There was a time when the Olympics celebrated the very pinnacle of athleticism and manhood. Running, fighting, chariot racing … that sort of thing. Naked wrestling. (Actually, that one I'm a little less keen on, but whatever.)

It's amazing to think how far at times we have veered away from the essence of the games themselves in today's modern Olympics. Now look, I'm not saying ballroom dancing doesn't come with its challenges—I mean, my God, the tightness of the pants alone can't be easy. Ron Jeremy would be the most entertaining participant and the most disturbing at the same time. But seriously, dancing? I would've liked to have seen the original Greek judges trying to decide if "Nick" had the proper arch in his back during his foxtrot. Something tells me Nick may have seen some large stones during the "Let's Throw Boulders at Those Who Can't Wrestle" event in Delphi.

And I'm going to be fair. This isn't about sports that suck. This is about events that don't really qualify as a sport. If it were about sports that suck, that's a different argument. Badminton, all types of diving, ping-pong, or anything with horses (except chariots)—these are events and activities no one needs to see. Even if you were hammered, it's impossible to think you could drink these sports good. But they do have an element of competition, and I suppose the ancient Greeks were probably diving and riding horses, when they weren't getting ripped abs. I know my history: I saw *300*. But I must apologize to Canada, because without diving and pony riding, we'd lose about 70 percent of our medal intake in the Summer Olympics. Synchronized diving? Isn't that something you do at the cottage? No medal ceremony in that case, just sore nuts. And this just in, we're now absolutely killer on trampoline, which completely validates my theory that if it's an event where you bounce (diving, riding horsies, etc.), Canada can win. Which reminds me, shouldn't Pamela Anderson have a gold medal?

Even as a kid, I remember seeing a container in the local variety store where you could put your spare change for charities like hospitals, African children, and—wait for it—the always-deprived Canadian yachting team. I knew something wasn't right. The Olympic yachting team? Yes, the hardships of trying to find the right ascots with the matching captain's jacket, or the expense of proper white sweaters to tie around your neck to impress Muffy after a hard day of drinking champagne and wearing sunglasses—how does one fund such a needy cause? Hey, Biff and Tad, beat it! Why not just ask Mumsies for the coin ... no Olympics for you!

When you think of some of the world's most popular sports that are not included in the Olympic Games—sports that have a lot of participation and interest, like baseball, rugby, or golf—you wonder about the criteria. What's up with modern pentathlon? As quoted from a pentathlon website, "The choice of the five diverse and unrelated sports that make up the Modern Pentathlon arose out of the romantic, tough adventures of a liaison officer whose horse was brought down in enemy territory. Having defended himself with his pistol and sword, he swims across a raging river and delivers the message on foot." WTF?!? Is this an Olympic event or a night at Gary Busey's house?

Is there another sport today that has grabbed the world's attention more than mixed martial arts? Trust me, if wrestling, the event that pretty much defined the heart of Olympic and human competition, doesn't make the cut, I doubt the overpaid elite of the IOC will allow an event that contains a "superman" punch. (Unless, of course, the MMA athletes are then to pick up swords that they will use to fight their way over a raging river, where they will find a horse on the other side that will take them to a ballroom dancing competition, where they will then deliver a message to a rhythmic gymnast, and then both of them will get on a yacht for a game of ping-pong.)

Look, anyone who can beat the best in the world at whatever it is they do is probably pretty good. I mean, by definition, they're good. I'm sure they work hard, and I'm sure they're talented. And I hope their parents are proud of their gold medals, I really do. And if you care about spelling bees, or jam-making contests, or three-legged races, well, I wish you all the best. But the fact that you and your friends like it doesn't mean it's an Olympic sport.

44 IT'S A FAN'S RIGHT TO SHOW DISPLEASURE WITH THEIR TEAM AT A GAME

Every time I sit beside some guy at a game and he starts to boo, I think he looks insane. I'm serious. It looks crazy. What does it do? Even the way you have to make that sound makes me feel uncomfortable. Lips all pursed, cheeks rosy, and your eyeballs popping out: You look like a blow-up doll is what you look like. (Speaking of which, who was the guy who invented the plastic blow-up doll and thought to himself, "Hey, I've done a pretty realistic job on the human anatomy here, because this is exactly what a woman looks and feels like." I always wondered about the guys who bought them: Did they know about Sears catalogues? Was there necking? Do you break up with dolls? What happens when you blow too much air into them—does their abnormally straight figure that so attracted you suddenly appear to be fat?)

To be honest, I've never been one to make very much noise one way or the other at a sporting event. Maybe I'm not a good example. I do yell. Yelling I understand, especially at an official.

And that just feels good. Let's face it, you're helping the team and I believe the team knows it! I think sometimes that one of the players might look up at me at that moment and think, "Hey, that guy in section 505, row 12, seat 26 is really giving it to that ref who blew the offside. He's got our back and this is going to motivate me. And he's not even spilling his rye and ginger! C'mon guys, let's go out and win for the guy who looks like Ted Bundy's angry friend!"

Look, I know what you're thinking. "I've paid my money and I can do anything I want"—right? That's what you're thinking? Maybe you're saying that because you hear players say something like that when a reporter asks how they feel about loud booing at home. Well, guess what? Those players are basically calling you a jackass. And that's not such a terrible choice of words for someone who thinks that buying a ticket to a sports game is the same thing as buying the right to deliberately insult a near-stranger.

I wonder if this is a result of knowing how much a player makes. If a fan has judged a particular player's performance at any given moment during the game as "undeserving" of the salary that he knows is being earned, that player can therefore be heckled, jeered, or booed. There is so much wrong with this idea that I hardly know where to start, so I'll just say this: News flash, the player doesn't choose his own salary. The GM does. I mean, if I could choose my own salary, I would. If I could pencil myself into the starting lineup of the Calgary Flames, I would. And I'd pay myself handsomely. But there is a reason teams don't allow that. So don't boo a guy because of his cap hit. He's just getting market value.

There is also the lack of civility—period—in the way we react to each other in everyday society, so why should it be any different for those who go to a game and pay a ticket price that is relatively expensive? Do they not feel they have a "right" to show displeasure for a "privileged" athlete who is underperforming? It is who we have become. We are the crowd at the Roman Colosseum, and after that interception, "Thumbs down to you, Sam Bradford! You have been weighed, you have been measured, and you have been found wanting. Off with his head!" Or in this case, "Booooooo! You suck!!"

By the way, how far have we come as a culture when the most common phrase you can use about an individual performance that has displeased you is, "You suck!"? And it's used for everybody and everything. The goalie sucks, the ref sucks, the offensive line sucks, the ice sucks, the building sucks, the field sucks. There is more suckage going on at a sporting event than at mead night at Caligula's Palace on a Saturday. And look who we're talking about. Dion Phaneuf sucks?! *Really?* I don't know, maybe you don't like Phaneuf. Maybe you don't like some of his decisions. Maybe you don't like the Leafs. But *sucks*? He's much closer to being a league all-star than sucking, I can tell you that.

People say Marty Brodeur sucks, or Roberto Luongo, or Kevin Bieksa, or whoever. See what these guys have in common? That's right, they're actually pretty great hockey players. Do you have to like them? No, you don't. But if you make the claim that they suck, I'm sorry, you're just wrong. (Just to be clear: If you're in the NHL, or the NBA, or the NFL, or MLB, you don't suck.)

Remember, "Root, root, root for the home team"? Are those days gone? I think they are.

And that is sad.

But is booing the best way to rally "your" team? Do you not cheer for them when they score? I just think when you play against a team that has a supportive fan base, you know it. It's deafening. And sometimes those teams can go a long time without being very good and they still make it a home rink/field/court advantage. Look at those who have gone to Arrowhead Stadium with painted faces, vintage jerseys, and giant headdresses to support their Chiefs, only to come home with makeup running down their faces like Tammy Faye Bakker after yet another horrific performance. It's because they "support" their team. It's why they keep going year after year. (Well, that and alcohol.)

That's just the cost of the good feeling you get when your team wins. Did you think you get something for nothing? Good gravy, no. The elation comes from caring *before* your team made it to the finals and the bandwagon got crowded. And the longer you've cared, the better it feels.

So, Oilers fans, keep your sweaters on. And Leafs fans, prepare for the best day of your life if the Leafs ever win.

45 THERE IS A "CODE" IN THE NHL

It's one of our most cherished national myths: Hockey players can police themselves, if officialdom would just let them. They respect each other so much, and have been so completely shaped by hockey's culture of accountability and fair play that if we could just get rid of the instigator rule, the only reason we would need refs out there would be to call offsides.

I've got to call it like I see it. Bullshit.

Maybe it was true decades ago. Maybe there were unwritten rules that governed the game. There may have been an understanding that players used to have for each other regarding a "right and wrong" code of honour that all skaters understood, beyond the rule book, the team, or the NHLPA. But if so, the erosion of this code of ethics that the players self-police is now complete.

It's been gone for at least the last five years.

Want proof? In the 2013/14 season, twenty-six players were suspended for either hits to the head or boarding. I'm not including pre-season, or other suspendable offences like slashing, goaltender interference, Shawn Thornton's fifteen games for "punching an unsuspecting opponent," or instigating a fight in the last five minutes of a game. I'm really just talking about the suspensions for things that would kill a player if he hadn't been wearing a helmet. Actually, there are incidents like that pretty much every night, but these are the ones deemed dangerous enough to make a guy sit.

Not that it seems to work. The trend is clear: Everyone is fair game. If Phil Kessel has to fight John Scott, or Nathan MacKinnon has to fight David Backes, I'm sorry, there is no code. (And seriously—why does a guy get a five-minute major for getting jumped?) If players are getting run over from their blind spot several steamboats after releasing the puck, just because some gorilla thinks he has to "finish his check," there is no code.

Fine. But hold on. What is this *code*? Well, it's unwritten, so no one really knows. But since everyone gets bent out of shape if someone takes liberties with a "skill" player, I think it's safe to say that the code is in place to protect scorers. (The whole beef with Steve Moore was not the hit, it was *who* he hit: Canucks star Markus Naslund.) The code seems to mean this: Thou Shalt Not Lay a Finger on First-Line Players (Maybe Second-Line Ones, Too).

The thing is, this is absolutely not hockey tradition.

Remember the olden days? Depends on your age. To some, that refers to a time when cell phones were used to talk on only. What? No data plan? Not 4G capable? I still remember when someone with a car phone was pretty impressive. Who was that guy, Robert Wagner? I know, I know … a *Hart to Hart* reference. What's next, quotes from *Quincy, M.E.*?

But when you think of the era of the Original Six, and those who played during that time, what do you think of? Those guys were *tough*. We hear a lot about how players today are so much bigger and faster. Maybe. But I don't think there are many guys in the league today who could go into the corner with Gordie Howe or Rocket Richard and come out with the puck. Sure, those guys were legendarily skilled players, but they were just as likely to punch or elbow somebody as they were to score a goal. Let's just say they had a lot of space out there.

Toughness, competiveness, and an ability to put the puck in the net—I think they had all of that, plus the stars of the game played a no-holds-barred style of hockey that meant you took care of yourself. Even the elite of the elite fought heavyweights. Anyone who dropped the mitts with Bobby Hull or Bobby Orr was likely to go home with a sore face.

Did that mean there was no code back then? No, just a different code. I think the code was this: You play the game at the same risk as everybody else. No one's special, no privileges for a perceived "higher" skill set, just the game. You can score all the goals you want, but if you tangle with the beast on the other team while trying to freeze the puck, don't be surprised if he takes it seriously. He's not going to give you a free pass just because you've never been in a fight before. No crying to the officials, no league review, no upset agents—just the game.

Come to think of it, equality is not such a bad idea for a code.

Anyway, the game has changed drastically since those times. The code then was a reflection of the trends in society at that time. Now, society has told us, "Your child is special!" Don't get me started (it's in another chapter).

So, yeah, today's code seems to be eroding. But maybe that's not such a terrible thing. Maybe it's not that players no longer respect each other—it could be that changes in the game are starting to reflect an earlier time. If hockey goes back to "every man for himself," I for one don't hate it. Down with the "special ones," I say!

If they don't like it, there's always tennis.

46 *TENNIS IS A GREAT GAME*

I'm told people say this. This phrase is supposed to come up in normal conversation with the "everyday" person. But who really talks about tennis at a dinner party? I know who: no one. And there's a reason.

When we were young, tennis was a game played in the summer at the park. Those were great days. Hitting the ball back and forth, killing hours in the sunshine, or, even better, grunting under the lights on a beautiful summer's night. As we got into our teens, some got a little more skilled, buying more sophisticated racquets and hitting the ball with more accuracy. We started to emulate the tennis stars of the day, fashioning ground strokes in their manner. You were that guy. You could feel everyone in the park thinking it!

You were magnificent. You were Björn Borg! (Well, that's what I thought.) Others of my day were Jimmy Connors or John McEnroe. Yes, men of personality and a sense of cool.

Also at this stage, tennis at the park brought another element into the lifestyle of the summer-park tennis star: girls. Why, who wouldn't want to be seen with you? A Donnay racquet with the grip made for two-handed backhands; cut off jeans, nice and tight, made complete with white knee-high athletic socks; a headband, but only if you had the hair to back it up. Ahhh, those were the days! And yes, "Tennis was a great game!" We all played it. A game of the people.

But that ended. No more personality. Names you can't pronounce. (Just how many consonants does a name need? And what is that letter with the line through it?) Country-club guys, who seem like they would throw a fit at the mere mention of someone calling sparkling wine champagne. As an example, this is Roger Federer, or some French- or Italian-looking guy, at an exclusive nightclub after a match: "Did you just set this glass down for me?" "Yes sir," the server replies. "What did I ask for?" tennis guy questions. "Champagne, sir," is the timid response. "THIS IS PROSECCO! AN ITALIAN SPARKLING WINE FROM THE VENETO REGION, MADE TRADITIONALLY IN THE AREAS OF CONEGLIANO AND VALDOBBIADENE, IN THE HILLS NORTH OF TREVISO! IDIOT!! HOW COULD YOU MAKE SUCH A MISTAKE?!" He would then turn to his Eurotrash entourage and say, "C'mon everybody, let's go from looking at me in this awful nightclub to looking at me in my limousine!" "Yeah," they would all exclaim—or whatever the equivalent is in Euro talk—storming by a crying waiter, who merely wanted to attend Carleton University and take their bartending course.

Pro tennis is boring. Hours upon hours of grunting between two guys devoid of personality. And, then guess what happens? Towel boys! Yeah, get this: They can't even wipe themselves! Why I'm sure Ilie Nastase never even bathed! And ball boys! Did you know these kids don't even get paid? What is this, Dickensian

London? Hey, jerks, just because you don't have any balls doesn't mean you can't move your overpaid ass and pick up a fuzzy yellow ball! Why Rod Laver used to excrete his own tennis balls when he ran out! No Kathie Lee Gifford child slaves fetching balls for that guy!

Let's face it, tennis is for guys who aren't any good at football or hockey. It's true. If they were good at something else, surely to God, they would not have chosen tennis. It's just not the manly thing to do! (Oh, and by the way, this piece was based entirely on the premise that we are talking about men's tennis. Not women's. That changes this entire argument. Women's tennis is awesome. I PVR all the events and then watch them late at night in the dark of my basement.)

47 YOU HAVE TO WIN CHAMPIONSHIPS TO BE CONSIDERED A GREAT PLAYER

It comes up all the time when we consider Hall of Fame eligibility. "Yeah, so-and-so could sure play the game. But how many rings does he have?"

There is no question that the best who have ever played a given sport were so dominant that trophies were all but inevitable. Some athletes are so extraordinary that they won multiple times. And we have descriptions for those people: "First ballot" and "living legend" come to mind. (How about Gordie Howe, who was playing in the league *after* being inducted into the Hall of Fame?) These guys are so good, they can't help but win. And if you're that good, and win that much, you get voted into the Hall of Fame. Simple. And who is the poster boy for the first-ballot Hall of Fame induction? You get one guess.

Did you name Michael Jordan? If so, you are right.

To lists MJ's awards and accomplishments is ridiculous. Google it some time when you want to kill a couple of days. If we are to look at stats to simplify Hall of Fame status, maybe the fact

Michael won NBA Championships in 1991, '92, '93, '96, '97, and '98 is a good place to start. What? Seriously? If some being from another planet, a planet of sports geeks, were to get hold of this interplanetary information, surely they would consider Earth to be a planet of liars or people who make terrible typos in their documents. Either way, I'm sure they'd call bullshit.

But Michael Jordan is in a category of his own. And guys like him ruin it for a lot of people. If the thinking is: Michael Jordan won a pile of championships, and he's in the Hall of Fame, then I guess you have to win a pile of championships to deserve a spot in the Hall of Fame. But there is another trait common among many of these extraordinary athletes who dominated their game. I would say that trait is the ability to make others around them better. How about Larry Bird and Magic Johnson? They may be the best examples not only of those who made others better but also of two athletes who literally saved a league and captured the imaginations of all sports fans in what can be considered a defining moment for the entire NBA. Oh, wait. They both won championships and hoisted trophies.

So what about guys who dominated and made their teammates better, but never won a title? Can you be considered one of the greatest players of all time if you haven't won a championship? Thanks for asking. The answer is yes.

In fact, there are those in halls of fame who haven't won championships. Karl Malone and Charles Barkley never earned a championship ring, and many would say they were unfortunate to play in an era where Michael Jordan roamed the courts. They weren't defined by the ultimate reward, and yet they achieved Hall of Fame status, which I believe to be justified. There are circumstances where great players, maybe even some of the greatest, played on teams that lacked championship talent, but that didn't take away from the exceptional careers those players had.

Will Steve Nash be considered one of the greatest who ever played if he doesn't win a championship? Did he not make everyone around him better by being on the floor? Does the accomplishment of being the MVP back to back in 2005 and 2006, and an eight-time NBA all-star during an era that included Kobe, LeBron, and Tim Duncan not qualify as great? (In case you're wondering, yes it does.)

Dan Marino may be the best example of player greatness without having a championship trophy to prove it. Whatever his teams may have lacked (running game, defence), his ability to carry the Fish never wavered. A trophy was not needed to define the brilliance of Marino.

Were Dale Hawerchuk, Marcel Dionne, or Gilbert Perreault not great? Was Borje Salming not deserving? Is anyone going to think Jarome Iginla wasn't a great player if he doesn't win a Cup? Are you kidding?

I'll go out on a limb here: I don't care whether you liked Eric Lindros, whether you thought he was a whiner or a cancer in the dressing room, or whatever. The Hall of Fame is not there to celebrate the accomplishment of being a nice guy with swell parents. It's there to celebrate the players who stood head and shoulders above the rest, and anyone who thinks you can step into the NHL as an eighteen-year-old and run roughshod over the best players in the world, and *not* be a special player is insane. Take a look at the record book. The only names ahead of Lindros's in several categories are Gretzky, Lemieux, Bossy, and Stastny. I think we can safely say the guy knew how to play hockey. (Plus he won an Olympic gold medal.)

I understand why championship trophies matter in terms of Hall of Fame criteria. But greatness should be defined beyond hardware, beyond rings and singular stats. For certain special athletes, they are the ones who defined greatness, changed the way in which the game was played, and made the game better for all sports lovers. And seriously, it's not like everyone who gets his name on the Stanley Cup goes into the Hall of Fame. You don't have to be great to win a Cup, and you don't have to win a Cup to be great.

48 THE NCAA SHOULDN'T PAY ITS STUDENT ATHLETES

I understand why people generally feel this way.

An athletic scholarship at a big-time college can be worth hundreds of thousands of dollars. A school shouldn't hand out money to those who have *already* had their education paid for by a scholarship. What, these guys want to be paid *twice*?

Full-ride scholarship athletes are spoiled babies who have never heard the word *no*. They need to just zip it, and get back to playing football. Am I right?

No, I am not. (But since I didn't really mean that, I am not wrong either.)

Sure, there are lots of spoiled, entitled babies on full-ride scholarships in the NCAA. But who cares? That's not the point. The *point* is that NCAA football alone will rake in $40 billion over the next fifteen years.

That's just the TV revenue, and yes, that's billion with a *b*.

The players are the engine of this enormous, cash-making machine. Last year, the University of Texas football program made

$104.5 million; Michigan, $85 million; Alabama, $82 million. That is business, not education.

The NCAA rules and regulations regarding player compensation were originally conceived when students went to school to *learn*. And the schools were there to teach. These student athletes were working for a better vocation and the chance for upward mobility when they finished school. Sports were a way to support school spirit and identity. (They also happen to be fun.) Back then, even pro sports were poorly paid. If the pros weren't doing it only for the money, it wasn't a stretch to ask amateurs to suit up for a pat on the back and a letter to stitch on their sweaters. (Plus a scholarship.)

As pro sports and salaries began to change in the late 1960s and early '70s, the function and importance of college athletics changed. In other words, they became moneymakers. The enormity of the bottom line and the drive for finishing number one, or appearing in a nationally televised bowl game, has taken over.

While the business has changed, however, many of the NCAA rules have not. Now the schools are in it for the money, but the players are expected to be in it for the scholarship. There is another name for that: exploitation.

The issue is far-reaching, and the answer complex, but the math is simple. The NCAA's revenue in 2012 was $872 million; the cut for student athletes was $0.

Stipends for players should be increased. It's not as though there isn't enough money to go around.

Perhaps you think student athletes lead privileged lives? And perhaps they do. But they worked for it. Just like any pro. And for many of them, it's their only shot. All those kids are dreaming of going on to pro careers, but to say that a full ride at a Division 1 school is a one-way ticket to the pros would be slightly inaccurate—as in 98.3 percent wrong. That's right. Only 1.7 percent of those players get to the payoff they've been working toward their whole lives.

The others don't get paid. But the schools do.

Now, this is not an argument about the validity of the education received by the student athlete or their seriousness toward finishing school. Yes, education is important, and players should make the most of it, particularly when the odds against turning pro are so massive. I'm not saying that schools should pay cash *instead of* offering scholarships.

The question is about fairness to those who sacrifice their bodies for the chance to play varsity sports and, in turn, create enormous revenue streams that benefit the university, its educational programs, and the community in which it resides. Is it okay to sell the name and likeness of a varsity athlete, and then condemn him when he receives free pizza after the game at a restaurant that is jam-packed because of his play? Should we be surprised when college players sell their championship rings for money when the pros do it all the time? Only when the billions of dollars the schools rake in don't trickle down to the players.

So yeah, by all means, the schools should cover tuition. But that's the bare minimum. There should be more for players whose hard work and sacrifice bring in the revenue. And I'm not talking about letters for their sweaters.

49 VANCOUVER IS A GREAT CITY

Canada is made up from such diversity that it is staggering to think we are all under one flag. Whether the criterion is language, geography, or architecture, Canada may be the most varied country on the planet, and it's what makes us great.

Of course, for all of our regional differences, we can agree on some important things. For example, everybody hates Toronto. That may never change. The centre of finance, the largest population, the highest concentration of imported cars, the Leafs. Look, I get it ... Toronto is *supposed* to be the place everyone hates.

But what's up with Vancouver?

Guess what, Vancouver? The rest of Canada is not so sure about you either. You used to be so sweet and quiet. What happened?

Not that you're all *that* bad. But please. You didn't invent the Rockies, so please don't try to take credit for the view. Same with the ocean. Be honest. You found the place that way. I mean, it's nice and everything. Don't get the rest of Canada wrong. But it's not like Saskatchewan is getting all high and mighty because they invented wheat.

While we're talking, Vancouver, we've got to address the topic of sports—hockey, actually. As in, the Canucks. It's a problem. Who are the most disliked fans in the NHL? Vancouver fans. It has even been written about in various men's magazines and blogs, including an interesting take by hockey blog writer Chris Richards of *The Province*. "Unwarranted arrogance, scumbag demeanour and crybaby antics [are] the most viable reasons to abhor the blue and green. And while I can't wholeheartedly disagree with [another critic's] assessment, I would have different reasons for the high ranking [of the worst pro sports fans], such as the constant bandwagon jumping, a sometimes pedestrian atmosphere at [the former] GM Place and the riots that follow Stanley Cup losses."

You're okay. We like you. We like your mountain and ocean vistas, but it doesn't define us as a people, the flag does. So what if the stars of your hockey team are Swedish twins? We all like Swedish twins (like you, many of us have paid handsomely for Swedish twins). I like Swedish twins. We don't need to hear about your fervour for running and swimming because there is a lot of it in this country. Moving down the list: a taste for fancy coffee, running, Pilates, Lululemon ... trust me, this stuff exists across the country. It doesn't make you special.

But hey, you don't need to be special, do you? Don't try so hard. Why do you want to be special anyway? (Oh, as for the rest of B.C., you can shut up, too.)

There. That's better. Now, I think you'll find that the rest of the country will be happy to go back to hating Toronto, as though this whole thing never happened.

50 *THE NEW ELITE ATHLETE IS THE TRIATHLETE*

When you take into account what triathletes go through in order to compete in their sport, it is almost overwhelming, if not unfathomable, for most of us. Have you seen an Ironman race? A 2.4-mile swim followed by a 112-mile bike ride, and then finished with the always-fun 26.2-mile marathon. What? Was the marathon on its own not torturous enough? Who runs 26 miles and says, "Is this it? Well, maybe I'll go to the gym."

And that's just the race itself. There's also the commitment of time, and it's enormous. Want to complete a triathlon? Try training five to six days a week swimming, running, and biking, and if you're competitive, you'll need to be watching distances and times.

Kind of makes you wonder why someone would invent this race. What, no cable? You enjoy pain more than Albert Fish? No chance with the opposite sex and tired of playing *World of Warcraft*?

That's not entirely a theoretical question, by the way. The

answer: Triathlon was invented in the early 1970s by the San Diego Track Club as an alternative workout to the rigours of track training. The club's first event consisted of a 10-kilometre run, an 8-kilometre cycle, and a 500-metre swim. Over the next decade, triathlon grew by leaps and bounds and soon gained recognition throughout the world. In early April 1989, the International Triathlon Union (ITU) was founded at the first Congress in Avignon, France, the very city that hosted the first official world championship on August 6 later that year. The ITU has maintained its headquarters in Vancouver since then. Triathlon was awarded full Olympic-medal status in 1994.

So, does all this make them great athletes? I think what it makes them is incredibly committed people who strive for excellence in physical fitness and stamina. I think individuals who are able to swim, bike, and run in a day what most of us have never done in a lifetime is exemplary. Bravo.

Does it make them the best athletes on the planet? Sorry, no.

When I think of what makes a true athlete, I think of the dictionary definition: "a person who is trained in or good at sports, games, or exercises that require physical skill and strength." Extraordinary physical fitness on its own doesn't make you an athlete. It just makes you fit.

My definition has always included the fundamental ability to pick up any sport at a level of excellence regardless of time spent playing or learning the game. Hand–eye coordination; peripheral vision; balance; explosive power; an aptitude for mind games; strategy; mastery of the leverage of body position; intimidation—these are the things that define the athlete. That's not to say that there are no triathletes who fit this description; I'm just saying that being a triathlete on its own doesn't ensure it.

I think the reality is that many of the participants in this sport never considered themselves an "athlete" before engaging in this activity. I'm guessing a significant percentage may not have been overly fit previous to finding solace in the event itself. Want to bet that a lot of triathletes start out after making New Year's resolutions?

Triathletes are more like bodybuilders than hockey or football players. They have mastered part of what it takes to be good at sports without being good at sports. Phil Heath, "Mr. Olympia," who has been on my show several times, is a natural athlete. When I asked him, "Are bodybuilders athletes?" Phil's response was, "Some are." But bodybuilding doesn't *make* you an athlete. Phil should know: He was a scholarship NCAA basketball player at the University of Denver.

This is not to put down or diminish the triathlete, but rather to define what I believe is at the heart of athleticism. If a football is thrown in the direction of a triathlete, would he catch it? Probably not. If he does, well, maybe he's an athlete. But if his nose swells up like Marcia Brady's before her big date with Doug, well, maybe not.

51 *THERE IS A TIME TO LET GO OF THE GLORY DAYS*

And that time is never.

There are plenty of good reasons to play a sport. Here's one of them. Maybe the biggest. Sports make you who you are. And why would you ever let go of *that*?

Not that you have to have accomplished anything huge. Think back to your earliest memory of your participation in sport. For most of us here in Canada, it's hockey. The experience from coast to coast is almost identical and helps make us who we are as a people. Early Saturday mornings, and I mean early. As a kid, the thought of 6:00 A.M. meant one of two things: Christmas morning or hockey. Dad taking you to the rink in full gear with the skate guards on. Remember that? For wee novice players, there was the half-rink with big wooden dividers at centre ice. Seemed logical—after all, there was another game taking place on the other side of the dividers. For many, the memory of their first goal lasts a lifetime. Do you remember yours? Do you remember the sponsor of your team? First coach? You bet you do!

How about high-school sports? For most of us, it seems like yesterday until you see a picture of yourself playing basketball or volleyball in a high-school yearbook. Did I always wear shorts like that? They seem, well ... uh ... a little snug. I look like an extra from the movie *Cruising*. John Stockton's got nothing on me. But reminiscing about particular games and moments from games is what keeps us close. "Hey, remember when Ross threw the basketball over his head, standing completely backwards to the basket with one second left to win that game?" "Yeah, I remember that. What a spaz!" "Yeah, what a goof!" "Yeah, what a loser!" See, memories are what keep us young.

I don't cringe when I hear other guys' triumphs, no matter how trivial the story might seem, although I draw the line at bowling, cards, or board games. I don't want to hear about great moments in Sorry or Clue. Who needs to hear, "Hey, remember when I guessed it was Professor Plum in the library with the wrench?!" No, I don't. Now go kill yourself.

There should also be a moratorium on fishing and golf stories. Just because. And it should be strictly enforced. Look, I enjoy hearing someone revel in the sheer ecstasy of how they flew one out of the trap in 1997 at Angus Glen, and then put a spin on it to "hole out" for a 71. I enjoy it once, maybe twice, but after that I'm throwing the flag.

So sit back and relax and enjoy the stories with the boys. Even feign interest if you have to, but just remember it's important to them and you might just learn a little something new from a friend or co-worker. Unless, of course, they start talking about great moments in Monopoly, then you have the right to start laying down the plastic in the kill room.

52 *THEY CAN'T HEAR YOU*

I often hear the comment, as if this was supposed to be funny at some point: "They can't hear you, you know." Oh my God, that's hilarious! But here's the thing: The yelling is not for them; it's for me. And for all the yellers around the world, we must unite, and condemn the "they can't hear you, you know" people! They will never know the satisfaction of completely blowing a gasket over what we perceive to be pass interference; or berating an official with a barrage of insults and demeaning innuendo, only to finally see that flag thrown into the air fluttering to the ground as if to acknowledge the tremendous foresight that I had in seeing the obvious foul before him. "Yes, well played," the official must be saying to himself as I toss a satisfied smile at the TV, giving it a wink and thinking to myself, "I do what I can."

There is also a wonderful and admittedly delusional understanding that the team on television not only needs my encouragement but also the excellent play calling I have going on at home. In my basement. By myself. For instance, when you're watching a football game, and the team you're cheering for is on defence, and the offensive team runs a draw, do you scream out loud, "DRAW!" I know I do, and the team really seems to respond. How often do you scream, "Time out! Time out!" All the time, right? Do you then look at the clock? Do you ponder how many time outs "you" have left? Yeah, that's right: you! Oh, you have called an excellent game, Mike.

And let's be honest, when you have a room full of men doing this—the yelling, the screaming, and the swearing—doesn't it feel good?! Real caveman stuff. And invariably, one of the boys is going to yell something out loud that he will have difficulty living down for a very long time. I once heard a buddy, in a fit of rage, scream at his team, "Get off the league!" What? Did I hear that right? What does that even mean? I always thought he was an English-speaking person.

I think yelling at the TV during a game is part of the "in-game" experience. If you can't be there live, just bring the stadium atmosphere to you. You want to see psychotic? Watching me during a game that really means something to me (that is, I'm gambling on it) is a study in the inability of a grown man to control his inner rage. Sybil has nothing on me. Once, a neighbour made a comment about the "apparent enjoyment" that my "friends" and I were having while watching a football game. "You guys made quite a racket for three hours. It must have been some game! You guys sounded like you were having a lot of fun!" I didn't have the heart to tell her it was just me. Awkward.

We all do it. Don't worry about it. How many times have you said something aloud, only to hear the announcer or colour commentator say the very same thing moments later and you proclaim, "Hey, I just said that!" Of course you did, and don't think the announcers weren't aware of it, either. You are that good. You are a part of each and every game that comes into your living room or pimped-out rec room. The players respect you, the networks embrace your expertise, and the coaches appreciate the help. So, the next time you run into one of those "they can't hear you, you know" people, just ask them, "Then why do they keep looking back at me when I make all these great comments and suggestions?" And when they have no response to that and just stare blankly at you, simply suggest that if there's any more interference while the game is going on, then they're going to get a letter from the "league." I mean the nerve of some people! Now, if you'll excuse me, I'm going to have to call a time out, as I'm getting low on rye ...

53 *THE WINTER OLYMPICS ARE FANTASTIC*

Sometimes, I feel like the Winter Olympics were created so snowy countries can feel good about themselves. Sort of like summer camp where the chubby kids don't win any of the sporting-type events, so there is an arts and crafts competition that allows the camp councillor to say, "Look, everyone … Timmy made a butterfly hat!" Timmy now feels good about himself, regardless of the looks he gets from the more athletic children, who are now clapping for Timmy, while they whisper under their breath, "Did you see the stupid thing that fat kid made?" "Yeah, I wonder if he's going to eat it?" "Ha ha ha ha ha!" "Yeah, ha ha ha ha ha!"

The Winter Olympics certainly hold some intrigue and there are incredible moments, but the rest of the world must watch curling and think to themselves, "Are Canadians really that bored? How clean do they need to make that ice? Didn't they play this game in the movie *Cocoon*?" Now, I like curling, but it's not like I'm going to explain this game to a football coach in Tennessee.

Biathlon might be the oddest of the sports, and it holds some interest because the participants shoot guns. But they shoot targets; and if we watch their breathing and cross-country skiing for way too long, then we wish they would shoot each other. I also think that these Nordic events are the one time that skinny white Danes and Norwegians are able to gloat—not unlike the quiet non-athletic kids in elementary school who hide during gym, but do the moonwalk when they win the math quizzes in class. Am I calling the Nordic Olympians nerds? Yes. But not the women: Some of them look great.

The X Games events have added a sense of cool to the Winter Olympics. Snowboard, snowboard cross, and other newer-type events have brought a strange vernacular to 45-year-olds. *Fakie*, *crooked cop air*, *corkscrew*, and *half-pipe* are all snowboarding terms: not to be confused with words some people used to describe Rob Ford. Still, if I ever saw one of the snowboarders on my property in the summer, I'm sure I would turn into Clint Eastwood, stare down the barrel of my shotgun, squint my eyes, and tell Shaun White in a steely hushed voice, "Get off my lawn!"

I get figure skating. I get the artistic side of the event and the enormous sacrifice it takes to perform the jumps and moves. After having interviewed many ex-NHLers who have competed on *Battle of the Blades*, they will tell you it was one of the hardest things they have ever done. But the judging has a history that makes presidential elections in Chile look legit. There is also way too much crying, far too many pale Russian guys who look like they got ousted from the legendarily mediocre hair band White Lion. And sports aren't supposed to have sequins. They just aren't.

So, here in Canada, we can still be proud of our excellent athletes, many who are now household names, and realize that the Winter Olympics team does a great job during the games. Just know that when the anthem is playing and our guys are getting the gold for the two-man bobsled, the rest of the world is clapping, while saying under their breath, "Did you see what those stupid Canadians just did?" "Yeah, I wonder if there is chocolate in those medals." "Yeah, I wonder if they're going to eat it." "Ha ha ha ha ha!" "Yeah, ha ha ha ha ha!!"

54 CANADIANS AREN'T BASKETBALL SAVVY

Canada: the opposite of basketball, am I right?

No hitting, no playoff beards, no fighting (and a good thing, too, given the number of basketball players who carry guns).

But wait.

Not only are Canadians more basketball savvy than ever, it appears this country is now reproducing at a stunning rate just to fulfill the quota of first-round draft picks for the NBA. Canadian national team officials are also identifying the country's top players earlier. Steve Nash Youth Basketball—the nation's version of Pop Warner football—has affected more than 25,000 Canadian children ages 5 to 13. And don't forget about the influence of the NBA in Toronto. Canada as a nation is starting to catch up internationally, and the future looks bright.

The one constant of any sport is to show its youth that you can win in it. Now, even though international victories have been slow to come, the vision of the North American youth, not unlike hockey, is not so much national in focus as it is professional.

Success is seen as a pro-centric goal as opposed to a national program result: NBA championship versus Olympic or world championship gold. In this example, Steve Nash is the poster boy for any Canadian who has aspirations in achieving American basketball success.

But where do you pinpoint the start? To me, the beginning of the Canadian invasion starts with the success of Leo Rautins. The former basketball star of St. Michael's College School in Toronto went on to play at Syracuse University under legendary coach Jim Boeheim, and then he became the first Canadian ever to be drafted in the first round of the NBA, by the Philadelphia 76ers. To see someone who actually played for the school you go to achieve such heights inspired many kids from the Toronto area to do the same. Public schools like Eastern Commerce Collegiate Institute and Oakwood Collegiate Institute became powerhouses and stars like Jamaal Magloire began to emerge; in fact, current Canadian NCAA stars credit Jamaal as a major influence on them.

With the growth in Canadian participation south of the border, the level of basketball also increased at the CIS (Canadian Interuniversity Sport) level. Canadian championship "final fours" became a draw on national TV; in particular, some fantastic finishes took place at Saint Mary's University in Halifax. But the true measure of Canadian progress in basketball can be seen not only in the number of recruits who are showing up in big U.S. programs but also in the significance of the roles that they play on their teams.

Anthony Bennett, Tristan Thompson, Kelly Olynyk, Cory Joseph, and Joel Anthony—these are just some of the names that not only played but also starred in big NCAA programs. And perhaps the biggest star from north of the 49th parallel is just around the corner: Andrew Wiggins. There is huge excitement in Canada about basketball, and with it comes a more sophisticated understanding of the game. I still think that, internationally, our best days are ahead of us. Wouldn't it be something to see an all-star-laden basketball team of current NBA giants donning a red Maple Leaf on their tops?

There was a time when there were a lot of jabs sent our way as Canadians when it came to our perceived understanding of basketball. "Don't play in Toronto; the fans don't understand the game." Well, they're wrong. Dead wrong. The Raptors fans are great, and they have turned up when the product may not have deserved any support. With some great drafting, maybe there could be a chance for a championship. Imagine that! Now, imagine if the star of that team went to Newmarket High School or Henry Carr Catholic School in Toronto? Now that would be cool ...

55 *YOU BECOME MORE REALISTIC AS YOU GET OLDER*

I suppose if everyone matured at the same rate, becoming more realistic with age would be considered a natural progression of life. Unless of course, you're a guy. In which case, what you believe to be true at the age of 18 should still be true years later.

Injuries almost always occur because males carry the "we think we can" gene. It is part of the little-known group of male genes that also includes the "jump up and touch the top of a door frame" gene; the "I don't need directions, I know where we are" gene; the "I can handle my liquor" gene; and the "watch *Scarface* and *Braveheart* over and over again forever" gene.

Being realistic isn't fun, nor does it inspire. Was it realistic that James T. Kirk would wave a "universal language translator" so he could understand giant-headed blue people and gorilla monsters that resemble white unicorns? No, but we have that now. Dick Tracy, talking and seeing people at the same time via his watch: we have FaceTime. Think about the most male-dominated movie genres, like science fiction, action, anything with James Bond, Arnold Schwarzenegger, and they are filled with innovations like voice recognition, face recognition, and any other imaginary gadget that makes the movie cool and the life of the hero easier. And guess what? We made it happen. Because, as we know, most men see themselves as their own version of a superhero: not a good one, but one with powers nonetheless.

See? Being realistic is overrated.

Superpowers that we ordinary, everyday men possess, that to some women may make us appear to be somewhat delusional, *are* powers: the ability to wear mirrored sunglasses on a beach to stealthily look at the girls walking by—they don't even know they're being watched; scoring a goal in old-timers hockey and believing if there was anybody in the stands, they'd be talking about that amazing goal ... these things may not seem like superpowers, but they are "strong with the Force." Going to a business lunch with other men and convincing yourself that your playful and suggestive quips to the waitress are somehow slowly making her fall in love with you. (Ever been to an Earls or Moxie's? This superpower is bouncing off the walls everywhere in those places.)

In fact, sports fandom for men is truly a drug—a drug that allows us to look at a five-year veteran quarterback, an all-American from Florida and a two-time Pro Bowler, and upon watching an incompletion, actually say, "What I would have done was ..." What? Just let it go. Of course, you would have done it differently, except for the fact that you never played, you are 5'4", 128 pounds, you're afraid of the colour orange, and the only trophy you have is for attendance. But once again, as we men get older, we let that kind of logic just float away. Are you going to redo the roof of the house by yourself? Of course you're not, but to the other guys, you can say that stuff out loud and we nod our heads in approval. Because we'd all do the same.

How many times will you hurt yourself in the gym trying to lift twice what the 24-year-old beside you just put up, just to show him "here's what a man lifts"? (For me, this is a common occurrence that has resulted in many walks of shame out of the gym, grimacing and trying to hide that I'm hurt, only to go home and cry like Jan Brady because Marcia got the guy again.)

But don't fret, men! Being realistic is for other people ... you know, like wives. Let them balance the books and make the decisions on vacations and home renovations. For you have much more pressing issues on your mind, like running around the block so neighbours can be amazed by your physical fitness, winning your fantasy football league, and standing in front of your big-screen TV when Sidney Crosby misses a breakaway to explain, "What I would have done, was ..."

56 THE MONEY IN PRO SPORTS ISN'T JUSTIFIED

A lot of people think that athletes are overpaid. They're wrong. Athletes are paid exactly what they're worth. Well, that may be open to debate. They may be underpaid, after all. It could be that the owners are overpaid. But the athletes? Impossible.

Want to know how I know? Because fans keep paying them. If fans really didn't think Shea Weber, or Aaron Rodgers, or whoever was worth what they're getting paid, they wouldn't pay to watch them play. But they do. Fans could watch something else, or nothing at all. But they don't. In fact, revenues keep going up.

Whenever you shudder at an amount of money an athlete receives, just ask yourself this: How many people can do what they do? How many people are willing to watch it? The fact is, sport and the professional athlete are held in the highest regard around the world. When people get upset at the dollar figures spent on sports as opposed to "worthwhile endeavours," they have to realize that society dictates what is worthwhile, and the verdict is: Watching Prince Fielder hitting a home run has been deemed to be more valuable than public education or a decent medical system.

It may not be fair, but we have decided that there is more of a monetary value in a puck-moving defenceman than an excellent teacher. Maybe that's appalling. But it's not hard to understand. It's supply and demand. Only a tiny fraction of us are going to be able to play pro sports. And everyone in that small group is therefore going to get an unbelievably huge piece of the pie. Or, to put it another way: What's easier to find, a good accountant or a 6'6", 312-pound offensive tackle who runs a sub-5.0-second 40?

Now, I think what bothers people the most is how the money that these athletes earn very often gets squandered. Not only is it tough for the average person to comprehend what $100 million looks like, but it's also well nigh impossible to understand how you could lose it all. Making bad decisions with money, however, is not the same thing as not deserving it. Once again, you couldn't deny at the time why Allen Iverson, Lawrence Taylor, or Mike Tyson were able to acquire such enormous amounts of cash in the first place. And, hey, all you had to do to get just as much money was beat Mike Tyson in a boxing match. How hard could that be?

In order for the money to slow down, the thirst for professional sports would have to reflect a decline in the interest of people who want to see someone dunk a ball, throw a touchdown, or score a hat trick—and I don't see that happening anytime soon. We live in a time where a man who eats 69 hot dogs in 10 minutes, in an event that's shown on ESPN, is considered a competitive athlete and part of the International Federation of Competitive Eating (IFOCE). I believe that there is *nothing* people won't pay to see, and on top of that, call it "sports."

Should you be appalled at what top big-league athletes make? Take a look around the globe. Phil Taylor made over $1 million playing darts in 2010! WHAT? Are we to understand that spending all those hours in pubs is actually worth something?! But here's the rub: To all those who pay to watch him play, to the many levels of sponsors who plaster the venues with signage, and to the television networks who broadcast his matches, he's worth it. The money is justified because there is hunger for what he does and those who will pay for it as consumers. What, did you think that people are paid in proportion to their contributions to society? Really? I mean, that's not true in *any* field. Why would it be true in sports?

Here's the secret. You wanna make the kind of "cake" that Phil Taylor takes home? No problem. All you have to do is beat him. Oh, wait. You can't. And that is all the more true in the big sports. These guys invest everything to get there. Those multi-million-dollar contracts are open to everyone. In fact, teams are always looking for someone to sign one. The trouble is, there aren't nearly enough people to hand them out to.

So, sure, maybe money for pro sports is out of whack. But we put it there. No one gets paid according to their contribution to society. They get paid exactly what society is willing to pay them.

57 MEN CAN HAVE CATS

No, they can't.

It's not an argument. It's weird and sad, and the only cats men could have would be like giant tigers or something and we all know how that ended up for Siegfried and Roy. (Although I'm sure the tigers, after having to put up with those two Halloween freaks for years, just decided they'd had enough of the accents, the fake faces, and the riding around on tricycles through hoops of fire.) Here's what you do if you're a man and you have a cat: Take your cat and look in the mirror. Does it look right? Do you think it accentuates some part of your persona? Don't you think you look like Dr. Evil? Somehow, I would imagine it's hard to pull off the "walking around with a live ball of fur" look, unless you live in a castle in a remote part of Romania and you're surrounded by vampires. Of course, if this would attract Kate Beckinsale, then I'd be prepared to reconsider.

I like animals, but I'm not a freak. Dogs are fun. I have one. His name is Reilly. We love him, but he's a pain in the ass. Most animals fall into one category for me: meat. Now, just so I'm not confusing anybody, there is an obvious line to me between *family pet* and *entrée*. If you have a pet that you can also envision being on the dinner table at Thanksgiving, then you fall into the Jeff Foxworthy category of "you might be a redneck ..." I'm told pigs are great pets, but I'm sorry—they're bacon.

Cats always give you the impression that they're thinking, "Oh God, I've heard that joke a thousand times and it's still not funny." We have wives, parents, and girlfriends who already have that job. I don't need Morris giving me the same attitude. You tell a dog a joke—and it doesn't have to be A-list material—its tail's a waggin', there's a lot of rolling around and hind-leg bouncing. Oh man, he thinks you're just killing it! He's the drunk crowd at a golf tournament dinner.

There is also the litter box thing. Gross. At least Reilly has the presence of mind to alert us if he has an extra deuce that was not taken care of during the walks. His subtle tapping on the door is a doody alert. He's not proud of it. I believe the scratching on the door is a little embarrassing for him, as if to say, "Look, I know you're comfortable right now, dressed in your reindeer pajamas, lying on the couch, just ready to watch your recording of *Boardwalk Empire*, but I really must 'crank an eight ball' that was previously unbeknownst to me. Terribly sorry, old chap."

Food. Dogs eat almost anything and it seems, at least by the commercials I see on television, that cat food is prepared by chefs. Some of them are French. What a step down that must be for a Parisian chef, when he discovers he won't be working with Daniel Boulud in New York at db bistro moderne, but, rather, as head meat masher at Mr. Mittens. And how about the look cats give when the food is actually laid out: hmphff. How can a man deal with that, after a hard day of cutting down trees, jackhammering concrete, and lifting whiskey barrels onto trucks? Enough, I say! You wanna be known as the cat guy, go ahead, but remember: What do they always find in the house with all the crazy people on *Hoarders*? What is the favourite pet of serial killers? What do lonely girls have? That's right, and now you've fallen into the category of "cat guy." Congratulations! Table for one? Welcome to Lonely Guy Town, population: you.

58 *BADMINTON IS A SPORT*

Badminton sucks. It's terrible. Don't argue its merits because there aren't any. If you are absolutely horrific at sports, then badminton is for you. Nothing looks more effeminate than playing this lady sport. I don't care about their so-called stars—there aren't any, and if there are, I bet recess was a terrible experience for them in elementary school. Crappy little wispy racquets, tiny and dainty courts, and the main object used in this activity is called a *shuttlecock*. What? You shittin' me? And to make it more manly, you're gonna call it what? A *birdie*? Everything about this game blows. Ever seen the individuals who play this? They look like the group of kids who were on the losing side in *Lord of the Flies*.

The game originated in the mid-1800s in British India, created by Brit military officers stationed there. If you're not feeling that all these ingredients combined isn't leading to a game that sucks, I can't help you. Being particularly popular in the British garrison town of Poona (now Pune), the game also came to be known as poona. Yeah, poona! Bwa ha ha ha ha ha ha ha! Now, this name is as close as badminton has come to actually attracting a man to play it. "Hey, Steve, wanna play badminton?" "No." "Hey, Steve, wanna play poona with Sally?" "Yes."

You know who is good at this sport? China and Denmark. I know: the two most natural enemies I can think of. I guess it all must have started with the Sino-Danish clashes during the mid-1300s, also immortalized in the movie *Clash of the Titans*, where Liam Neeson, who plays Hans Christian Andersen, defeats David Carradine's character, Kwai Chang Caine, in a deadly game of badminton.

And let's be honest, it's yet another racquet sport, but this one is for those who consider tennis to be far too frightening. Good crikey ... hey, badminton people, just take your embarrassing little "activity" and put it where it belongs: the backyard. Yeah, that's right, there beside other games, like horseshoes, that are social and yet aren't mistaken for real sports. I love playing horseshoes on a hot day. I never get confused about what it is: a game that is usually played by people who are hammered, with a cocktail or beer in one hand and a horseshoe for hurling in the other. Most times, you will hurl more insults and obscenities than shoes. This, in turn, is sometimes followed by other "hurling" by those who thought amaretto, grenadine, and Sprite made for a nice drink in the hot sun.

But here's the crazy thing: Badminton is a so-called Olympic sport! (Don't get me started on the Olympics again.) Let's do everyone a favour and have the world leaders just cancel this activity, in some formal protest at the U.N., as an "unsavoury attempt" to woo the unathletic into believing they were doing something that made them popular. How many guys brag at a bar or party at how great they are at badminton? Answer: rhymes with *schnever*.

59 COLD-WEATHER FOOTBALL IS CLASSIC

If you live in Canada and are a CFL fan, there are many games now considered classics that have been played in snow or icy conditions. Some Grey Cups, like the Ice Bowl in 1977 between Montreal and Edmonton, stand out—the Alouettes came up with the idea of putting staples in their shoes instead of cleats, and had a decisive edge in their 41–6 win. In the 1996 Snow Bowl Grey Cup held in Hamilton, the game featured a Toronto Argonauts team led by the legendary Doug Flutie versus a high-octane Edmonton Eskimos squad. This Grey Cup final was error filled, including a controversial fumble, with the final verdict going the Argos' way, 43–37. There are also NFL, NCAA, and CIS moments that have been played in wintery conditions.

I dislike all of them.

I want to see the best teams with the best athletes and the best coaching play in conditions that allow them to display their skill set and greatness. I don't need broomball shoes, staples in soles instead of cleats, "hot packs," or any other arctic-style improvisations to make a football game interesting. Adversity is a part of football. Rain, wind, snow, lousy field conditions, and ice are elements that do happen in northern climes where football happens, but is it great football? No.

It is football that pushes the endurance and ingenuity of a team and staff, but it isn't ideally the conditions I want for a game, let alone a championship. Very often, you will hear announcers and broadcasters talk about "what lengths" a team will have to go through to be successful during a given game where the weather is not ideal. Well, how is that going to accentuate performance? How about we do that to other sports where you want to see the best at their best? "Here we are at the world track and field championships, ready for the Olympic 100-metre final featuring world-record-holder Usain Bolt, where he'll run shoulder to shoulder with Yohan Blake and Justin Gatlin. The shovels are still making out the lanes through the snowdrifts here in Nunavut—temperatures today will exceed minus –45 degrees Celsius. Yohan Blake has reportedly put staples in his shoes, but it shouldn't matter very much, as we all expect them to die within seconds of the starter's pistol going off ..."

People will say, "It's great to watch." Really ...? Top-notch athletes with numb hands, balaclavas, bad attitudes, and frozen tears begging for the game to be over so they can go back to South Beach? Anyone see the unseasonably cold and snowy 2010 Sun Bowl in El Paso? Another instalment of "Catholics vs. Convicts" (Notre Dame vs. Miami) was one of the saddest bowls ever. The moment the "U" walked out of the tunnel shivering, the game was over, and sadly, the last game of my brilliant six-game parlay. The Hurricanes looked like a bunch of abandoned Chihuahuas that had been dumped on the side of the road during January in Moose Jaw. Sun Bowl, my ass.

Historic games in Minnesota, especially during the Bud Grant era, are very much romanticized. The Purple People Eaters, running after frightened quarterbacks slipping in the snow. People there loved the wintery snow-covered football so much that they built the Hubert H. Humphrey Metrodome.

Let's put it this way. Remember the snow at the Leafs–Wings 2014 Winter Classic, when no one could stickhandle or pass? Or the arctic temperatures at the 2003 Edmonton–Montreal Heritage Classic? Now, how would you like to see Game 7 of a Stanley Cup final decided under those conditions? Ridiculous, right? So why is it okay to decide football championships in the brutal cold?

So the Super Bowl was played between the Seahawks and Broncos at MetLife Stadium in New Jersey in 2014. The football gods smiled, and the weather conditions were fantastic for that time of year. Even Tony Soprano could have continued to bury bodies by the river with no difficulty digging. We were spared watching a terrible game in bad conditions. We just watched a terrible game in fair conditions. Sorry, Payton, maybe next year ...

Give me Miami, San Diego, or even New Orleans with the booze, sin, and vomiting, but please give me a championship that doesn't have the announcers repeatedly saying, "Well, it's definitely warmer up here in the booth! Ha ha ha ha ha ha ha ha!"

60 *SHOPPING IS NOT FOR MEN*

Fine. This one is not exactly *wrong*. Shopping is certainly not best for men, *but* shopping with a woman is not the hell on earth most sitcoms and movies portray it to be. I have done some of my "best work" while shopping. Remember my very helpful notes earlier on how to get women—well, here is an ingredient that was left out: Shopping is an aphrodisiac for most women. And, I have to admit, watching the one you have feelings for whip clothes on and off all day gets the ol' eight cylinder going pretty good, too! You ask, "But Mike, what if I hate shopping?!" Learn to love it, damn it. I'll teach you some magical ways to make this happen.

Booze. Mix in sexy little drink breaks, but make sure you make them romantic. Shop for a couple of hours, then hit a café, bistro, or restaurant for a little drinky. Once again, follow the playbook: Prosecco = good. Perhaps a little exotic nibbly as well, as this keeps the "date" fun and prohibits the "I don't feel very good" sentence that will ruin all your hard, and slightly shallow, work.

Imagine yourself as the Richard Gere character in *Pretty Woman*, perhaps minus the millions of dollars, the looks, the charm, and the limousine, but it doesn't matter—as long as *she* feels like the Julia Roberts character. Not that I'm saying you're in love with a prostitute. I'm sure your girl is lovely, and not exchanging sexual acts for money. And let's be honest, if you were in love with a prostitute and she laughed like Julia Roberts, wouldn't you want your money back? Let's just say that if I did want to pay for a prostitute for an entire week, I'd pick Cindy Crawford. Wait a minute, what was I talking about? Oh yeah, shopping ...

There is also something to be said for taking an interest in your significant other. Does she go to your slow-pitch ballgames, support your crappy old-timers tournaments, or tolerate poker nights with your cronies? This is a nice and easy way of saying thank you, with the added benefit of little or no talking. That's right! With shopping, there is a lot of head nodding and smiling. If she asks you, "Does this look good?" Don't think about it, just nod and smile. Repeat: nod and smile. If she asks about size, don't panic—just go with the lower number.

GIRL: Maybe I need an 8. What do you think?
YOU: I thought a 6?
GIRL: Oh you!

Whew, good answer. Now, on to the next store. "But wait," you say, "what about a little stop at this bistro for a Pinot Grigio and a chocolate croissant?" Wow, look at you: The student has become the teacher.

And don't forget about the ultimate two-way gift: lingerie. Now don't blow it by asking her to try things on, as that is a rookie mistake. And don't look at the hot chicks working there, because you are there with Julia Roberts (Cindy Crawford) and she is the only woman you see. You've come too far, worked too hard with all the head nodding, the croissants, the smiling, the wine, and the faking of dress-size knowledge.

And as you drive back from the day out, you will notice she is all smiles and for you that is the ultimate moment of happiness. That and the fact that as you look subtly down at your iPhone, you see that Florida State scored one more touchdown to cover the 52.5! You, sir, you are a god.

61 YOU CAN RECORD LIVE SPORTING EVENTS FOR LATER

Although I'm sure there are circumstances where one is not able to watch a game live (e.g., wedding, funeral, work, sex, etc.), under almost any scenario imaginable, it is unthinkable that you could enjoy a live sporting event, well, not live. Keep in mind, the having-sex example, as we all know, trumps any and all situations. If a man has a chance of any sexual activity whatsoever, it supersedes all other schedules or demands, including work, funerals, and possibly sporting events. A cleverly planned encounter, however, can take into account halftime, preview shows in between games, and a team historically being either a slow starter or a comeback king. There is also the option of attempting to watch while being somewhat engaged, but I would not suggest this. The suggestion by some oft-told jokes that certain positions will allow you to both watch sports and remain active, although amusing, is quite frankly reckless and dangerous. Such stunts are performed by professionals. Please do not try it at home (unless you have money riding on the game).

If you think that in this day and age, should you attempt to record a game to watch later, you can avoid the discussion of a score, well, good luck with that! In olden times—you know, the 1980s—if you were *taping* a game, really the only way of finding out an unwanted score was by running across a blabbermouth listening to the radio or inadvertently walking by a TV during the sports segment of a newscast. All very avoidable things. Now, the pitfalls and hurdles are formidable. Facebook, Twitter, sports apps, sports radio, TSN, and, as always, blabbermouths. There's nothing like going to tweet out the reason you hate the *Dexter* finale, only to see that Beebs86 can't believe the Lions gave up a late touchdown and they "suck balls." D'oh!

But the real heart of the matter is this: Live sport is the most important thing in the world. There is no excuse for not being available. A recital? C'mon, you know as well as I do that regardless of whose child it is—your sister's friend of the family's, or cousin's best friend's babysitter's—the kid will be terrible! Any one of them. Zero talent. Think of kids drooling over the playing of the always-wretched "cat and spoon" melody, or something equally annoying. Or an 8-year-old interpreting *Faust*: It all sucks. During my nephew's rendition of *Death of a Salesman*, I booed. His interpretation of Willy Loman was shallow and without believable despondency. And don't get me started on dance recitals! Horrific recreations of timeless classical numbers that most men wouldn't watch, even if Mikhail Baryshnikov was performing them in our backyard.

You think you should be at your aunt's funeral instead of watching a Game 7 semi-final, in which every previous match has gone to overtime? Let me ask you this: What's your aunt's mom's name? Where was she born? What was her maiden name? Do you even know this woman?! How dare she get in the way!

Maybe plop a Samsung 65-inch 1080p Smart LED TV right on top of the casket, and now we've got something going! Probably the first time ol' Aunt Agnes was interesting in her whole life anyway. Or was it Aunt Ethel? Whatever.

The lesson here is priorities, gentlemen. Look ahead, plan ahead, and always have a contingency plan. Someone dies, have a brother or look-alike in the wings. Rotate the attendance and you'll be fine. If work gets in the way of a game, know what illnesses you have used and store them in your smartphone. Now as far as the sex thing goes … well, do the best you can, and maybe, just maybe, you meet that mystical woman from the dirty joke and you get both. I know, I know, crazy—but a man can dream.

62 CANADIAN HEART EXISTS ONLY IN HOCKEY

I think for many Canadians, our heart is most on display when we play the game of hockey. It is something that we're proud of and, historically, it has defined us as a people and as a nation.

Playing on a broken leg; getting stitched up on the bench; Patrice Bergeron playing Game 6 of the Stanley Cup final with a separated shoulder, broken rib, torn cartilage, and a *punctured lung*. That sort of thing.

Scotland has Braveheart. We have hockey.

But to say hockey is the only thing that defines our heart as a country, that to me is inaccurate. Now before I am accused of being anti-Canadian, let me just say that as a native of this country, my heart was grown and nurtured by the game of hockey. Most of the finest men I have ever met were forged from the sacrifices they made in coaching me and others like me in the small town of Stouffville, Ontario. I would never give up the experience or the invaluable lessons that I learned from some truly wonderful people who gave me the best childhood a Canadian boy could ever have.

But as I grew up and experienced different people and sports, and travelled beyond the borders of Ontario, I realized that there is a lot more to defining ourselves than just a stick and a puck.

Lacrosse: I can't tell you how much I respect the guys who play this sport. You want to talk about heart? They don't have salaries that make the headlines on *SportsCentre*; they have part-time jobs and careers. They are some of the best-conditioned athletes you will ever see and you don't want to mess with them, as they play one of the most, if not *the* most, physically demanding sports on the planet. So what makes them by definition so Canadian? Nicest guys on the planet. Yeah, how about that? Great athletes, humble individuals, can kick the crap out of you if they wanted to—and still will buy you a beer. How Canadian is that? Plus those who coach, manage, and, to a huge extent, fund and own professional lacrosse in this country are nothing short of amazing.

A colleague of mine happened to be in the company of some South African fans during the 1995 Rugby World Cup, where Canada faced the home team as the heavy underdog. The way he tells the story, the South Africans were gloating before the game even began. And to be fair, the Springboks were favourites to win the tournament. But the advice my colleague gave the fans would have been more useful to the South African players. "Just don't run up the score. The Canadians won't respond well to that." Well, the Springboks were known as the toughest team in the game, but when one of their players took a cheap shot at a Canadian player, and the inevitable dust-up took place, it was the

South Africans who limped off the field bloodied. The game has gone down in rugby lore as The Battle of Boet Erasmus.

Our women in the 2010 Vancouver Winter Olympics were nothing short of extraordinary. Not only did they compete at the highest level and win, but the dignity, charm, and humility with which they handled themselves was one of the proudest moments I had as a Canadian. These athletes train virtually unnoticed for years, and sometimes will recede from the public eye once the games are over, but their commitment and determination to accomplish their goals in lesser-known ski and snowboard events is inspiring.

I think one of the most stunning examples of Canadian heart I have ever witnessed came from the Canadian women's national soccer team, which won bronze at the 2012 London games. Christine Sinclair might as well be Paul Henderson, Bobby Clarke, and Phil Esposito all rolled into one. Despite the heartbreak of the previous game against the United States, which was refereed so poorly (the ref could have been a French figure skating judge), the Canadians went on to get a gutsy win in the bronze-medal match. Canadian fans wouldn't have blamed the players if their heart wasn't in it. But that is the point: They were all heart.

63 THERE'S NO GOOD REASON TO MAKE FEMALE BAR SERVERS WEAR KILTS

After doing some tremendous and exhausting research over many, many years, I can tell you that kilt-wearing girls are big trouble for the male species. And here's what is more disturbing: It never wanes or weakens. You'd think that the power of the "kilt-wearing girl" would dissipate with maturity, wisdom, and a certain amount of knowledge that with age a particular style of skirt can no longer retain your attention. Nope—we become Benny Hill. But what is it about "that dress" that confuses and pollutes the mind of the ordinary man?

Is it the schoolgirl thing? Well, you can try to avoid the obvious perv implications of obsessing over a schoolgirl uniform, but if it weren't true, the movie *Exotica* would never have been made. If it weren't true, a lot of Japanese websites would be out of business, not to mention the makers of certain Halloween costumes. Ever been driving down the road, trying not to look at some of these "girls," and wind up almost taking out fourteen garbage cans? No, me neither.

I also think it goes back to some early feelings we men have about that whole "just above the knee" thing. It's the premise that showing less makes us want to see more. Although I don't believe the same feelings apply to the turn-of-the-last-century women's swimsuit. And why do the women pictured in those photographs always look like either Rita MacNeil or Alice from *The Brady Bunch*? Something tells me had they tried *Girls Gone Wild*, it might have been a lot of women with low self-esteem looking into the camera and saying, "Does someone want to see Ethel's calf?" Followed by a lot of bonbon eating.

I remember a particular volleyball championship I played in, held at St. Robert, the first Catholic high school in York County. Our school was dominant in that sport and the team was coached by my father, who had not lost a championship for eleven years straight at that point. (I believe he hit fifteen years in a row before he retired and probably won, in total, well over twenty-five in his time. That was just volleyball—he won at everything he coached.) The biggest problem for the team: The St. Robert girls came out in droves to see this dynasty. Good Lord and Jesus … it was all I could do to concentrate on just serving the ball. I'd never seen my father call such a quick time out. I had already been with the team to the OFSAA (provincial championships) once the previous year, and I had won an MVP as the team setter twice—but this was a tough situation for us to deal with. The next year, I returned to high school for a "victory lap." I wanted to transfer to St. Robert; my dad said no. I returned to Stouffville High School and won another volleyball championship. It was my third senior championship in a row. I graduated at the age 26.

Okay. So I have fond memories of wholesome young Catholic ladies who wore kilts each day. But I'm guessing that not all patrons of pubs whose servers wear tartan have the same memories. Nor would I argue for a moment that I'd feel differently if I were Protestant.

So don't be embarrassed by the kilt. It's part of the great "arousal" family: schoolgirl kilt, candy-striper, French maid, cheerleader, naughty secretary, and drunk toll booth woman. (I apologize for the last one. I don't think it's a thing. It should be.)

64 COFFEE HOUSES ARE GREAT HANGOUTS

Remember coffee?

Not sun-dried Sumatra Rasuna. Not the shade-grown, organic, free-trade Maui Mokka. And certainly not the Kopi luwak, thank you very much (the coffee bean that passes through the digestive tract of the Indonesian civet before being roasted and brewed. I wonder what *that* tastes like.) I mean coffee.

Want a laugh? When you get to the front of the line at your local fancy coffee place, look at the barista and say, "Ahh, just coffee." Then watch the look on the barista's face. "Ugh, we have the blah-diddy dark-roasted blah, or the decaf Himalayan blonde blah-diddy blah ..." You get the "you're-not-in-the-cool-club" look, while the server's coolio eyes roll behind those pretentious-looking "smart glasses." One time I screamed out, "Hey, who here went to the KISS concert last night?" I think one girl started crying.

It wasn't always this way. If you are of a certain age, you may not even know what I am talking about: the classic doughnut shop. A place that served two important things: doughnuts and coffee. That's it, with variations of the doughnut world, sure: the eclair, the Danish, cookies, some pies and tarts—but that's it. Plus coffee. If you wanted, hot chocolate was available, plus soft drinks and milk. Plus coffee. It's the way God intended the doughnut shops to be. And the part nobody talks about: plus smoking. And lots of it. I'm not a smoker and I certainly understand the dangers of it, but there was something soothing about the locals talking away, while a middle-aged woman asked if you'd like a jelly doughnut, all the while surrounded in billowy smoke. I think it actually made the doughnuts taste better. I miss the classic doughnut shop!

Doughnut shops had real names, like Mister Donut, Donut King, and Winchell's. Dunkin' Donuts has tried to hang on to its roots, but the pressure of fancy coffees, European snotty syrups, and the worldwide smoking ban has made them a dying breed. They also had bubble gum machines, classic diner stools, and, yes, cigarette machines.

It seemed like one day, all this disappeared. In place of the old-school shops, we now find sleek espresso machines, Wi-Fi passwords written in haiku form on chalkboards, and crowds of hipsters ignoring each other while they gaze at their iPads. Gone is the possibility for locals to sit around and chat, so there's no place now for Gladys and Reggie to catch up. No. Today, ol' Gladys and Reg would have to buy laptops, then bring them into the java lounge, hog all the seats and spread out like they were in their own living room, and spend hours being assholes doing nothing.

Where are the doughnuts? Okay, Tim Hortons—I get it—but what about a doughnut shop? (Seriously, though. Panini? This is dangerous territory for a doughnut shop ...) Have you seen what's on display now at Coffee Temple? It's like a pastry museum with baked creations behind bulletproof glass. You point at the French chocolate whatever it is and nod at the coffee sommelier like you're picking out a lobster at a high-end steakhouse. Then they ask you what kind of coffee you would like. Have you looked up at the eye chart? Is it English? Will I get this wrong? All of a sudden, there's a lot of pressure and nobody is smoking. It looks like a scene from *Logan's Run*, and I think they all know that there is a flashing light in the palm of my hand!

I say someone should attempt a chain of throwback doughnut shops! You know, something like Donuts and Smokes, or "Just Coffee and Donuts and Meat." Get back to the old days—a time when a cruller came with a smile, some change, and nicotine.

65 *THE BORN-AGAIN ATHLETE IS A PHONY*

Maybe it's because we live in the age of the televangelist, but there is a real discomfort when an athlete professes his relationship with the Lord. We just can't help letting a tone of mockery seep in when we talk about a football player who publicly admits his strong feelings about Christianity. I think most of society, due to the exposure of many high-profile religious zealots as hypocrites, is highly skeptical of those who make such mighty declarations based on their spiritual beliefs. It seems so many tele-charlatans, who claimed to represent one church or another, invariably cheated on their wives, ended up in hotel rooms with hookers, and/or swindled people out of their money under the guise that contributions to the ministry were helping others in need. It's a shame, but we should admit the truth—we paint them all with the same brush.

Tim Tebow, the phenom out of Florida, became an obvious target for such ridicule. I should know, because I made fun of him, too. A persona I created showed up on *Mike Richards in the*

Morning every week, misquoting scripture, talking in an overly excited voice, and ultimately ending up crying or swearing when God failed to descend from heaven to help him win the game. I know for many, the distinction between the characters I create and the actual human being is sometimes misunderstood. I take a basic impression, use the voice, modify or exaggerate characteristics, and create "my version" of a public personality. *Saturday Night Live* and *SCTV* did this for years using the same principle. The Mike Richards's "Tim Tebow" is just that.

What was lost, perhaps, is that I believe he may be one of the most sincere Christians who ever walked a football field. There was the time a writer tried to catch Tim off guard so as to capture the "real" Tebow. When the writer landed at the football facility in Denver, Tim was nowhere to be found. He was at a soup kitchen, helping at a mission. He doesn't tell anybody, and there's no publicity. It's who he is.

Maybe the greatest example of those who practise what they preach is Michael "Pinball" Clemons. Pinball is a self-professed born-again Christian, and yet there is no overt preaching, no cornering an individual to "witness," and absolutely no judgment thrust on others. He is one of the finest human beings I have ever met and is one of the greatest examples of an athlete *in action* this country has ever known. If ever there was a person who led by example, "the Pinner" is the standard by which every athlete should measure himself or herself.

You would think there'd be an appreciation for those people in professional sports who live by their beliefs that promote the betterment of their fellow competitors and respect for others above themselves. Isn't it strange that those from the sports world who often dwell in the underbelly of society, embracing drugs, guns, and violence, sometimes receive less scrutiny than those who say, "The Lord is my Saviour"?

I wonder if here in North America we have reached such a level of cynicism that the Christian athlete will never be taken at face value again. We have seen the erosion of faith in our public schools with the abolishing of the Lord's Prayer, the replacing of the word *Christmas* with *holidays*, and, seemingly anywhere there is a connection to the Christian Bible, the deeming of it as unfair by other factions in society. (Try pushing this kind of doctrine in some other countries. Good luck!)

I think there are many athletes who are great examples of true Christian qualities, and they often get thrown under the bus because their personal beliefs aren't considered sincere. I just hope that we haven't lost the ability to recognize the solid human beings from those we wouldn't invite to a Christmas party. Sorry, make that a *holiday festive gathering*.

66 *ALL ANNOUNCERS ARE THE SAME*

Think about it for a minute. Who needs someone to tell you what you're seeing? I mean, in the olden days, when we listened to sports on the radio, I can see why you'd need someone to tell you what was going on. But once sports appeared on TV, why didn't we just watch? Who needs Bob Cole and Harry Neale to tell you what's happening right in front of your eyes?

Let me answer a question with a question. Ever watch sports with the sound turned off? It's almost unrecognizable.

To me, the craft of play-by-play is still magical and mysterious. How can you nimbly and quickly paint the picture of a series of immediate actions that can be so unpredictable? How do you create a story in real time? How do you find just the right word/phrase? (Or invent it—thanks to the great Danny Gallivan for giving us "cannonading drive" and "Savardian Spin-o-rama.") How do you even get the names right?

No two announcers are the same, and the great ones

crystallize moments so that most of us can recall them like it was yesterday. It is amazing how a voice, a turn of phrase, or a description can immediately transport an individual to a specific moment in time. The voice of an announcer can transcend what could be considered just a sporting event, creating an emotional connection—it can become a part of your own personal history. Depending on your age group, you might be thinking of different great sporting moments right now. I would say for many of my generation, the Foster Hewitt call of the 1972 Canada–U.S.S.R. Summit Series has never left our souls. The voice, the emotion, and the overwhelming sense of drama rings in our heads: *"Here's a shot! Henderson makes a wild stab for it and falls. Here's another shot, right out in front ... They score! Henderson has scored for Canada!!"* As I'm writing this, I'm welling up again. Damn it ... happens every time. Hewitt was brought out of retirement to do the '72 series; and regardless of some mispronunciations of certain players' names (even some Canadian ones), our lives were forever changed by his play-by-play work.

And how about the local guys. Vin Scully, who has been calling Dodgers games since they were in Brooklyn. That's right. He's been with the team since 1950. Jack Edwards, who calls Bruins games, is so obviously biased that he chirps at the other team. Rick Jeanneret loves the Sabres so much that he goes hoarse cheering when they score. Whether or not you like the Bruins or the Sabres, see if you don't get goosebumps when these broadcasters call a goal. And let's not forget the colour guys. I mean, who could possibly forget Daryl "Razor" Reaugh likening a Jamie Benn end-to-end rush to "poop through a diarrhea-infected goose." I'd like to forget it, but I can't.

For me, Don Wittman brought Canadians some of the top athletic moments our country has ever achieved. Wittman's track and field calls with his great friend, the effortless Geoff Gowan, quite simply were the best on the planet. Very few broadcasters in the history of sport have been able to deliver the detail and emotion the way in which Don verbally painted a picture. Donovan Bailey, the Atlanta 4 x 100-metres men's relay team, and Ben Johnson were all stories within themselves, but it was the magic of Wittman's description that made them "personal" for all Canadians. Let's also not forget NHL hockey, the world juniors, curling, and perhaps my favourite, the CFL. To this day, Witt's calls of some of the most dramatic moments ever in the Canadian Football League live in my heart.

Dick Enberg calls everything that moves. There's a reason for it: He is fantastic. There is a humanizing of sport that magically takes place when he calls an event. I still have difficulty understanding how he makes tennis, baseball, football, basketball, and Olympic events all sound equally exciting. His calls of NCAA basketball, college bowl games, and his ubiquitous "Oh, my!" roll over me like a comfort blanket. His calls are legendary and so is he.

But what about those who don't call the play but host the events? How do you separate the voice and presence of Canada's own Brian Williams from some of sports' greatest moments? The reality is that he almost single-handedly has delivered into our homes the most important stories in the history of Canadian sports in television broadcasting. Whether in our living rooms, kitchens, or bedrooms, Williams was counted on to deliver the news to Canadians, both good and bad. He is more than just a sports "presenter," and he has very few peers that I can think of. I suppose Williams is our Jim McKay, Walter Cronkite, Brent

Musburger, and Bob Costas all rolled into one. He is our historian. How he never ages is beyond me. But I do know one thing: His work has changed the lives of Canadians forever. His history is our history.

Announcers make a difference.

67 *TORONTO NEEDS AN NFL TEAM*

For many years, the question was whether Toronto could possibly get an NFL franchise. And for years, my answer was no way, no how. But with different names involved in a rumoured attempt to bring the Bills to Toronto, I now think the answer is yes. The names potentially involved in the process, like Jon Bon Jovi and Tim Leiweke, bring something to the party that did not exist before. They have connections, they have resumés, and they have access to cash and construction. The NFL is, and always will be, an old boys' club. It is the model that they have created and that model has grown the business into a multi-billion dollar juggernaut. Bon Jovi knows everybody, especially those who "count," including Robert Kraft of the New England Patriots and Jerry Jones of the Dallas Cowboys. He's also American—and America loves Jon Bon Jovi. He has cash. If Larry Tanenbaum is involved, he has cash and MLSE knows they could take care of stadium needs. This could happen.

So now the question is, should it?

This is not about the CFL versus the NFL. What game is better? Who has better talent? Those arguments are fruitless.

The only question I would have for Toronto as the marketplace is whether or not the "culture" of football is strong enough or sustainable. For years, there were people who believed that even if you had a scrimmage in Toronto with NFL players, people would just burn their money to see it. We have come to know that this isn't true. The Bills-in-Toronto experiment has been a dismal failure. This is not so much an anti-NFL bias as it is a case of the Buffalo team not being a playoff contender. The matchups have been boring, and the current-day citizens of Toronto are no longer wowed by an NFL logo. There is no emotional attachment or involvement with the team from western New York. The reality is that Buffalo doesn't give a rat's ass about Toronto and Toronto doesn't care about Buffalo.

I also happen to think that, overall, the Greater Toronto Area and southern Ontario don't make up a real football community. It's the cold, hard truth. There are pockets of CFL fans, and those who profess their love for the NFL, but for the most part there aren't "football people" in the region. University football, unfortunately, is mostly ignored in the area. You may not think so, but if you compare the GTA to almost any U.S. region, this is not even a conversation. There are parts of Canada that exude grassroots football support, have strong high-school programs, and hire top-notch university coaches. These pockets of the country are populated with families that have played for generations, from bantam and minor football all the way to university, *and they go to all the games*. But guess what? Saskatchewan won't be getting an NFL team. Neither will Alberta nor Quebec. Toronto is the only candidate, and don't tell me Ontario is a football province! Next thing you're going to tell me is that you've been a

York University football season-ticket holder for the last twenty years.

When it comes to the conversation of possibly bringing an NFL team to Canada, the Toronto question has gone to the next level. The business model and those involved *could* make it happen; the real question is, after the billions of dollars that would be spent acquiring the team, building the stadium, and putting a team on the field, will the people of the GTA be prepared to support football for the long term? How long could they suffer through losing seasons and still go through the turnstiles? Is the generational worship we see for the Maple Leafs something that could occur through osmosis in the GTA for NFL football, making it viable? Based on what we have seen with the Bills experiment—viable, yes; solid business move, not so sure.

68 *IT'S NOT PERSONAL, IT'S JUST BUSINESS*

Strangest and most inaccurate phrase I've ever known.

You hear it all the time in sports and in business—and it just irks me, or makes me laugh, when I hear it. Can there be anything more personal than telling someone how much they're worth?

As many "money" people will tell you, "it's how you keep score." If that's the case, and especially if you are a competitive person, how can a low number *not* be considered the ultimate insult?

I think the tying of the personal to the business end of things also became increasingly sensitive when the NHLPA allowed the disclosure of salaries in the early 1990s. Agents could then determine what their client's paycheque ought to be by comparing it to another player's position, statistics, and performance. So it's not personal when a pro athlete finds out he is getting a lower salary than Poops McShittington? Trust me, it's personal.

The phrase, "It's not personal, it's just business" must have come from those who were cutting the cheque. But both sides know it's personal. That's one reason agents exist. Sure, the agent is a professional negotiator. But many organizations would prefer to deal with an agent than the client. Why? Because any comments made about a player's performance, and criticisms a client may make of management, are buffered, and therefore hurt feelings are (the parties hope) kept out of the negotiation process. If business wasn't personal, then why do 98 percent or more of the professional athletes in the world have agents?

That's why salary arbitration is such agony. Suddenly a player has to listen to the team he's asked to bleed for pull out a list of all his shortcomings. He says, "I think I play like so-and-so, and he makes $3 million. So I'd like $3 million, too." And his GM says, "Are you kidding? You think you're as good as so-and-so? Get real. Here's $1.5 million. On a two-way contract."

Being told you're not as good as you think you are is not personal?

How about a lowball offer? The ability to "bring home the groceries" is a term I have heard a lot in describing what becomes important to those looking for a paycheque. In the negotiation process, a lower offer for the employee/player is seen as an insult to the way in which his family life is being viewed by the organization. Less money equals less respect. Negotiations enter the realm of optics at this point. Rarely is an organization not respectful of its employee's family life, but then again, that's why the business end for an athlete or anybody else *is* personal. Money, salary, and wages are directly tied to self-value. In sports, there is a minimum salary, but not minimum wage. Scales change and everybody wants to be considered for an increase should the scale go up for another individual you believe you are equal or superior to.

How about trades? Players always put on a brave face when the reporters come to talk with them as they're clearing out their lockers. "We all know that it's part of the business," they say. But do you think it doesn't sting? The team you just took a puck in the face for is now saying, "You know what? We're getting rid of you because we think the team is better without you. We know it may be inconvenient for you to move to a different city on a moment's notice, and unpleasant to tell your wife it's time to sell the house and move, and to pull the kids out of school. But we don't care." Sorry, there is no way that's not personal.

Of course it's personal. And it's personal because it works the other way, too. Guys try harder when it's personal. They play for pride, for their teammates, and for the crest on the front of the sweater. Just listen to the kinds of words used by Kobe Bryant, after his most recent contract signing with the Los Angeles Lakers: "It makes me want to run through a wall for them," Bryant said upon inking a two-year, $48.5 million deal. "It kind of just adds more fuel to the fire of being able to come out and kind of prove to everybody that [the Lakers] are right and everybody else is wrong."

That's not a statement about monetary gain and financial stability, or that the dollar figure was a good business move. It was about "proving everybody wrong." And this is Kobe Bryant. Still, after all these years, all the championships, the MVPs, and the already enormous amounts of money made, Kobe is attaching his self-worth, his person, and the respect for his character on the dollar figure the Lakers give him. Don't tell me it's not personal, unless, of course, you are cutting the cheque. Then it's "just business."

69 CHRISTMAS EXCITEMENT ENDS WITH AGE

You would think with the cynicism that comes with age and the years of unwanted carolling, the busy shopping malls, seven thousand turkey dinners, homemade pants as gifts, and constant driving to relatives' homes that Christmas would now feel like an unfair judge's prison sentence. If you had a lawyer pleading your case, he might say to the jury, "Ladies and gentleman, this man has been giving gifts for 45 years; been forced to drink a milk concoction with cinnamon, rum, and eggs; assembled 250 electronic cars, castles, and Lego sets; and been forced to sit on the lap of a strangely dressed, overweight man on twelve occasions while his parents took pictures! I say enough, ladies and gentlemen, enough!" Ultimately, everything should add up for all those over the age of 35 to detest Christmas, but you'd be wrong. Christmas brings a feeling that just doesn't last long enough. I love it.

I think there is nothing warmer than having family and friends, all together in one house, indulging in food and drink and talking until you can talk no more. As you get older, the social aspect far outweighs the "so what did you get?" question. I'm always amazed when I hear an adult ask this question. What are you, 12? And let's be honest—men don't ask that question. Maybe it's because 98.7 percent of the television ads from November 1 until Christmas Day are geared toward children and women. As men, we must make them happy. This is why during the holidays, there is extra male drinking, and in general, as long as you have provided the wife and children with the correct understanding of the "wish list," you get a pass on the boozing. How many times have you heard this? "Daddy's being funny!" No, Daddy's hammered. As is Uncle Steve and Uncle Claude and Uncle Scott and Mommy knows that she is probably driving home tonight. Fun for Daddy is over tomorrow, but tonight, Daddy is living like it's his last night before the electric chair.

I never tire of the little ones freaking out over their Christmas morning presents, because as you get older, you know that the same child who couldn't wait to wake up at 6:00 A.M. to see if Santa filled his stocking is now the university student who you need to wake up around 10:30 to convince him that unwrapping socks from his great aunt holds the same excitement as getting the Xbox One. My son and I both know it's different. He looks at me. I look at him. His mother is now looking at both of us. Damn it, son, open the socks—the Xbox is coming, just don't set her off. I head for the kitchen for another round of mimosas … Daddy need drinky.

I also like to see snow at this time of year. I know, I surprised you. I'm not doing any activities in it, but it just looks nice. Sometimes I hear people saying, "I don't need snow for Christmas. The original Christmas didn't have any snow!" Sure, and also during the original Christmas, they didn't have any indoor plumbing or vaccines to fight plagues, but I think we're all in agreement things might be better now. There are other things that are better now, too—fewer stonings, TV, lots of rooms at many inns (some with indoor pools), and Baileys.

Aside from my wanting sometimes to end people's lives in busy shopping-mall parking lots, Christmas truly is the best time of the year. Fellowship, best church services of the year, smiling grandparents, and a chance to forget about work all make for the healthiest of human environments. Oops, I almost forgot ... bowl games. Thank you, Lord, and may the East Carolina Pirates cover the –3.5 in the MILF.com Bowl. God bless us, everyone!

70 YOU DON'T NEED STARS ON THE TEAM TO WIN

Spock: "The needs of the many outweigh the needs of the few, or the one." Okay, okay, so Spock technically didn't play sports, except for that episode in which both he and Kirk had to go to Vulcan because Spock wanted to mate, since Vulcans mate every seven years, but when he couldn't get laid, Spock fought Kirk in a WWE/UFC kind of way. While technically not a team sport, I think we can all agree that there actually is competition on Vulcan. And that Vulcans would be good team players.

There are a lot of sports adages about team and teamwork. Even some of the most famous and iconic sports figures in history have quotes attributed to them espousing the importance of teamwork. Michael Jordan: "Talent wins games, but teamwork and intelligence wins championships." Vince Lombardi: "Individual commitment to a group effort—that is what makes a team work." I have always understood the team concept extremely well as an athlete, a coach, and a professional in my current field. Teamwork makes a big difference. But what is evident is that a hard-working team with the "blue collar" workmanlike ethic is great, until it meets another team with the same work principles but also laden with superstars.

There have been instances over the years where those who were truly blessed with natural athletic ability were lazy. Their attributes were so much greater than those they played with and against that the idea of trying to improve was silly to them. (Mario Lemieux on off-season training: "After August 1, I don't order fries with my club sandwich.") But today's superstars, for the most part, work very hard on fitness. Many aim to be the first on the ice, court, or field and the last one off. And when these mega-stars turn it up, all the hard work in the world by a lesser-skilled opposition can't stop them.

There are different terms for the "gifted ones." The term I like the best comes courtesy of one of my favourite people on the planet, hockey analyst Pierre McGuire. He calls an athlete with awe-inspiring talent "all-world." That term sums up just how few players of that elite ability there are, and should there be an exertion of effort by these individuals at any moment, oppositional defence may be futile. Sometimes it may also be a level achieved by a special player for only a given period of time, which is why I find comparing players of different eras a difficult discussion. But one thing is clear: If you have one, or God forbid two, of these players on your team, you're probably winning championships.

Who is all-world? In basketball, LeBron James, Michael Jordan, Magic Johnson, Larry Bird, or Kareem, to name but a few, and they could all change a game single-handedly, regardless of who else was on the court. They were part of a team that *they* made better. In hockey, Wayne Gretzky, Bobby Orr, Mario Lemieux, Guy Lafleur, Sidney Crosby, and certainly other names, but they all are or were game changers who elevated their teams to greatness. The reality is that the superstars get the big cheques because of their ability dominates games.

An average-to-good athlete can work hard and be an integral part of a team. If you find enough good players with a common goal who work together to create a well-oiled machine, you will have a chance at great success. But if you want to win championships in pro sports, you better get out that chequebook, write in a big number with lots of zeros, and make sure that superstar becomes a long-term investment. The New England Patriots are an excellent team, with a brilliant coach, and a whack of Super Bowl wins, but take away Tom Brady and all you have is an excellent team. You need stars to win.

71 *NEWER MUSIC IS JUST AS GOOD AS PAST MUSIC*

Ever wonder why it is that in a world of relentless change, no one can seem to come up with a better breakfast cereal? I mean, new ones come and go, but basically we're still eating the same ones we had when we were kids. Same with chocolate bars. From generation to generation, we see the same stuff in our kids' Halloween bags as we got. Are the candy engineers just not trying, or is this just as good as it gets?

If it were merely Mars bars, I wouldn't be too worried. But why can't anyone come up with better music?

It has always been a generational argument that the current music of the day is never as good as the music that preceded it. How many times have you heard someone older than you, upon hearing a sampling of the latest music, jump into a lecture about how great the music was during their time and how the music of today has gone "downhill"? Every generation since Mozart has argued about whose music is better. In our time, there always seems to be some weird hippie or ponytailed intellectual who is more than happy to blather on for hours, telling you in great detail why today's music is a shadow of its former self. So here's the problem: I think I have just joined the hippie-ponytail guys. Today's music is wretched. It sucks. Blows monkeys.

I watched a live performance by Garth Brooks from the Wynn Las Vegas hotel. He stood on stage for two hours with just himself and a guitar. No band and no backup. Once again, this was live, as in live across the world, broadcast on CBS. Not live to tape—live. He went through his musical influences growing up, all the genres of music that influenced him, and then played snippets of those songs. The genres covered came from everywhere, such as old country, rhythm and blues, folk, Motown, and rock and roll. The variance in music was amazing and foregrounded a significant fact that really hadn't dawned on me before: Today's generation of musicians have been given a much more limiting background in music due to the formatting of contemporary radio.

Since about 1985, consultants in radio have made sure that the scope of what kids can hear is very targeted, and therefore extremely narrow. Pop music in the 1960s, '70s, and part of the '80s contained dance, rock, crossover country, R&B, and whatever music fell into what was deemed "popular." It didn't have to "fit"; it just had to be liked. The Rolling Stones didn't sample their music, and neither did the Temptations, the Eagles, Elton John, or Aerosmith. The theme song from *The Sting* was a hit in the 1970s! That was ragtime, for crying out loud! Contemporary commercial radio of the time played it! It charted right up there with the Spinners, Bachman-Turner Overdrive, and Kool & the Gang! Pick your influence, future musicians—it's coming from everywhere!

Here's a scary thought: There may be a generation of children who might have Justin Bieber as a "musical influence." What do our kids have to base their musical influence on? A really limited choice of sampled music that has more to do with the marketing of a bunch of pouting little crybabies and "wannabe actors" as opposed to true musicians who want to rock their audiences.

That's why people still listen to Led Zeppelin. If we can't do better than an Oh Henry! bar, there's no way we're going to beat "Whole Lotta Love."

72 CANADIANS ARE JUST LIKE EVERYONE ELSE

After all the interviews I have done, the places I've travelled, and the characters I have run across in my business, I've realized that one stereotype is very true: Canadians *are* nice. Maybe some people don't like the image, but what is the problem with being the citizens of a country perceived as being the most pleasant on the planet? I'm always uncomfortable when people want to paint an entire culture with the same brush. When I hear others describe Americans, I always become uneasy, simply because the reputation is so bad. *Loud*, *obnoxious*, *pushy*, and *ignorant* are all words I've heard numerous times in describing our neighbours to the south. Is it true?

Well ... sometimes.

It always seems I'm trying to defend them on some vacation, going on a filibuster at a poolside bar, promoting what I believe to be the good qualities of my American friends, when some loud voice with an Arkansas accent spews out from the back, "Can I git some goddamn ice for my drink, Pedro?!" Thanks, Jed, there goes the argument. Election lost.

Sometimes I wonder what it is about Canadians that warrants our reputation—why is it so consistent around the world? And then I figured it out after being on a Mediterranean cruise during the summer of 2013. With about every culture from the planet Earth represented, I saw what had just been theory and conjecture put into practice. Canadians want to be *everyone's* friend. Not only that, but Canadians also want everybody else to be friends. We are the world's social conveners. We're "good-time Charleys," and yet polite at the same time. We are Richie Cunningham if he drank. We're the world's best man. We're Peter Parker. To the rest of the world, we're kind of like the TV show *Friends.* (But not the whole cast. If you really had friends like that, you'd become a serial killer.)

Meeting today's Canadian hockey players is a real eye-opener. In a time when there are a lot of evils to choose from, when the average NHL player is young and receives a paycheque that is generally in the millions of dollars, when hero-worship is at an all-time high, you would figure that dealing with these individuals could be unpleasant. It's the opposite. For the most part, I have found our Canadian professional hockey players to be affable, friendly, humble, and grounded.

You know why? They are very Canadian. The junior hockey players in this country who compete at the highest level are great kids, and I'm sure that they have made their parents very proud of them. And perhaps herein lies another piece of the puzzle: Some very committed parents are doing all the necessary things to help their kids succeed, and they're doing a pretty good job of being rocks for their children. Is this a trait that exists only in this part of the world? Am I saying Canadians are better parents than anywhere else in the world? No, not exactly, but the culture we have nourished for our children has, over the decades, produced individuals who are respectful of others, don't inherently believe they're better than anyone else, and, yes, maintain solid friendships. If there weren't truth in this, then why do some people travelling in Europe make sure their backpacks or luggage have Canadian flags on them?

Now I'm not saying every person from Canada *is* nice. Oh, we've got our fair share of dicks (as anyone who has driven in Toronto can confirm). But if there is one thing I'm proud of being, it's that I'm Canadian. I think we all are. Now let's go to your house, pour me a drink, and we can make fun of each other's favourite hockey players. Don't worry, I'll make the Timmy's run in the morning. For everybody. After all, I'm Canadian.

73 IT'S OKAY TO SCRUTINIZE COLLEGE ATHLETES LIKE WE DO THE PROS

Missouri kicker Andrew Baggett had a chance to send his team through to a third overtime against South Carolina during the fall 2013 NCAA season. He lined up the kick as thousands watched, then unleashed it—and watched in horror as it clanked off the upright. Never mind that Baggett had scored half of MU's points a week before in the Tigers 36–17 win over Florida. Never mind that he had kicked a 35-yard field goal to beat Tennessee in the fourth overtime the year before. His Twitter account lit up with comments about his ability, homophobic slurs, and one tweet that said "go kill yourself, everyone in Missouri hates you."

If you think that this is no more than an example of the things idiots say when they have the chance to be anonymous on social media, you're only partly right. Because our mainstream media spout idiocy, too. Maybe not quite as brutally, and not openly sneering. But we hold our elite junior hockey players up to ridiculous amounts of scrutiny, especially around the time when world juniors selections are being made. Yes, these are good hockey players. But they're just kids.

Sure, some of them get their tires pumped, but what about the guys who don't make it. What about kids like Angelo Esposito. Remember him? He was touted as a future number-one-overall draft pick and headlined as "the next Crosby." He was cut from Team Canada *three times*—each time with a camera in his face. I remember how bad I felt for the horrific treatment Esposito received in the press during the world juniors selection process. He endured criticisms of practically every aspect of his person, including attitude, fitness, ability, and heart. Within the coaching and scouting ranks, there could have been some legitimate concerns, but the way in which some media portrayed him on a national level was sickening. "Not Sid the Kid," was one headline. The blood was in the water, and our scribes went after him. He was 17 years old at the time.

When Esposito finally made the world junior team on his fourth try, and scored the gold-medal-winning goal while playing on the top line with John Tavares, to a man, his teammates said something along the lines of "good for him; I'm not sure I would have had the balls to come back a fourth time." They all knew that the media had made it harder for him than anyone else on the team.

It's tough to understand why some people go to such lengths to be so critical, sometimes verging on angry/sadistic. Quite honestly, I believe that jealousy comes into play a lot of the time. Petty, small-minded, and frustrated adults lashing out at teenagers because they perceive their targets to be privileged—the knives come out and let the decimation of character begin.

This for me is what I call a *hot point*. The lambasting of character that I hear at times from media and fans is disgusting and misguided. It is assumed that an athlete of a higher skill set, who has achieved scholarship status and perhaps national attention, should be under the same scrutiny as a professional athlete. There is a mindset that any athlete perceived as gifted, regardless of amateur status, should be able to "take it."

Those who have coached understand that there is a real line between expectation and projection. These are the two areas that divide the uninitiated and those who truly have an understanding of how to develop young athletes beyond just the skill set. Coaches who show great understanding of the balance between athletic accomplishment and the nurturing aspect of the coaching role are some of the finest human beings and would be successful no matter what they did for a living. Dean Smith, Mike Krzyzewski, John Wooden, Eddie Robinson, Bear Bryant, Brian Kilrea, and the list could go on, but they all exhibited the same great mentoring quality. There must be a mentoring aspect and a dignity in how we treat our children, regardless of athletic expectation. When a paycheque is received, then the pressures of adulthood will follow. Until that time, let's try not to "eat our young" before they have a chance to get started.

74 YOU KNOW WHEN YOU HAVE A GOOD BET

I wish I could say that I "knew" what a good bet was. The fact is, if I could catch myself at certain moments in my life, I would tap myself on the shoulder and say, "Look, I know you want to bet on the Lipscomb–Monmouth basketball game. Who wouldn't? But do you see they are playing the game in a tent? And why are you betting on Korean women's ping-pong again? You know last time Soo Yeon Lee burned you!" I have done okay with betting, but as mentioned before in these pages, it's the entertainment factor that I'm addicted to. Who bets on the French soccer league, hurling, Gaelic football, and the CFL all on the same day? Me, that's who. Is it sensible? No. But it's fun to bet on the unknown.

It's also tough to declare "a lock." Oh sure, there are gut feelings and, to a degree, some decent research that will tell you a given team is shite and will get pummelled by a very good team, but the bet is really the handicap or the spread. By how many goals? Are you using the Asian handicap (AH)? Can I sleep with your sister if the crap team keeps it within two? Okay, the last one technically isn't gambling talk for most, but what a wager! And let's be honest, should you go off the menu and bet on something you consider exotic, like a foreign soccer league? Let the buyer beware! I read Declan Hill's book *The Fix: Soccer and Organized Crime*. It's fascinating, and yet you will be terrified to ever bet on a soccer match again. What appears to be easy and "in the bank" may be exactly what the fixers/players/managers/owners/ syndicate are counting on you thinking. I'll still watch a match in Serie B and say to myself, or (to be honest) out loud, "Empoli, you lousy pricks! How are you tied with Reggina? You bastards!" Maybe I should have stuck with the Blackhawks at home to the Sabres.

How about those that venture into the wild world of over/ under or "the total"? There's nothing like two football teams that can't score to save their lives having kickoff returns back to back—after an interception—starting off a Super Bowl. Yes, I'm talking about the crappy Giants versus Ravens game in 2001. 34–7? If you had the under, you were gettin' a call from Nunzio.

I see all kinds of prop bets, but those don't interest me much. Coin toss, time of first goal, first team to be penalized, guy with longest surname to score, first fart, and all the national anthem stuff just aren't my cup of tea. Although, depending on the "artist," I understand the over can be a good bet for the U.S. anthem. Nobody seems to bet on "O Canada." I guess it's because nobody knows the words or the tune. Maybe we should make the Canadian anthem "Takin' Care of Business" by BTO. Look, if you can't figure out the words to this song, you've suffered a harder hit to the head than Gary Busey.

So don't look for the sure thing, because there isn't one. But should you find it, relish it, hold it, and never let that memory go, because most assuredly, the upset is waiting for you around the corner. Oh, yes … the upset, and then you'll find yourself saying, or yelling out loud, "Oh, c'mon, Juventus! You're losing to Catania?! You lousy pricks!"

75 THERE IS NOTHING BETTER THAN WATCHING CHILDREN PERFORM

I am a dad, from a family of teachers and coaches. My father was a brilliant educator, coach, and choir director. My brother Dave followed in his footsteps and works at a highly touted private school where he carries on in the family tradition of coaching and being involved with music and choral programs. My wife is an elementary school teacher. Parents love her. She is the type of individual who changes lives. If your child ends up in her class, you won the lottery. I get it. Kids are great.

But if I have to go to any of their school musical or drama productions, I will sever my leg like in a scene from *Saw* to get out of it.

I have collectively seen almost every kind of pageant, play, operetta, dance recital, Christmas program, Easter program, and musical performance that can possibly be performed on a stage. These productions are made possible only through the efforts of teachers, parents, and volunteers who dedicate hours of their time. I truly admire them for the sacrifices they make. But when

I see the indulgence and overreaction by the families that have children in the show, I long to be a member of the Hemlock Society.

Parents show up in droves, with camera equipment that even Spielberg doesn't possess. Grandparents leaning in to hear, uncles and aunts snapping photos, bored brothers and sisters, crying babies, followed by the third graders of Our Lady of Perpetual Motion in their five-hour performance of *Se7en: The Musical.*

Make it stop.

To me, there is nothing more disturbing than children singing adult-themed songs and having crowds go wild. Watching reality-based TV shows like *The Voice*, *America's/Canada's/Iceland's Got Talent*, *American/Russian/Haitian Idol*, and the original *Star Search* have these moments where some cutesy kid is belting out a song way beyond her years (or range), and the audience members lose their minds because little Tamara performed "I Touch Myself." Is it me? Isn't the creepy factor way off the scale? It's like watching the always-disconcerting *Toddlers & Tiaras.* White trailer-trash mamas dressing up their little 6-year-olds to look like Doutzen Kroes, and then freaking out on them because they didn't move their arms right during the *Moulin Rouge* number.

Enjoy your children's performances. It's true they do grow up way too fast and those memories will last a lifetime. But these performances are for you. Only you. Don't ask me to go. I don't *care* if little Esther is performing the lead in the fourth-grade version of *Hair*, I just don't have the strength to hear the destruction of music by those children who see themselves as the next Christina Aguilera. If I really want to be upset by children's performances, I'll just watch *Sportsnet Connected.*

76 IT'S RUDE TO LOOK AT SCORES IN SOCIAL SITUATIONS

Actually, this one isn't totally wrong. It's rude only if you get caught.

Are you telling me I can't find out if Kentucky and Kansas are going into overtime? I can't check to see if Drew Brees has made a comeback in the fourth quarter? Glance at Korean women's professional ping-pong to see if Soo Yeon Lee has burned me yet again?! Why is this such a social faux pas? What would I be missing? Have you heard the conversations at some dinner outings? "Well, you should see what Elliot made in class the other day. He took toilet-paper rolls and made them into binoculars! Right, Ted? Ha, ha, ha, can you believe that? Binoculars out of those paper rolls! Oh my God, we laughed! Ha, ha, ha ... And he's only 7! Can you imagine?" Yeah, that Elliot sounds like a regular Stephen Hawking. Holy shit, toilet-paper rolls into binoculars. What's next, a white sheet over your head to make a ghost?

I know not acknowledging others in a social situation is impolite, and to simply be engrossed with an electronic device while others are in your presence is insulting. This is why you must master the various techniques of sneaking peeks at your mobile, while not being discovered, and looking like you're interested in the conversation at the same time. First, have the games you need available "up" at all times. Scrolling is out. Always feign interest in the conversations that are around you as you may pick up on a random subject and offer the ol', "Hey, I always wondered where apple juice was made. I'll look that up on my phone right here!" Well played. And that will buy you plenty of time as you occasionally shout out comments like, "Some apples are better for juice, like McIntosh!" Heh, heh, heh, Brees has just put the Saints up by three. That's a cover. "Northern Spy apples are good for pies!" Don't showboat.

Some easy and obvious ploys for surreptitious game tracking follow here. Use the washroom—number 2s are acceptable and no one, publicly, can question you. Just don't use it more than once in an outing: that's just embarrassing. Forget something in the car and announce, "I've got to go get something from the car!" Just make sure it's real or something that people will believe; don't bring back a Cutting Crew CD and say, "Here it is!" Offer to get something from the kitchen. You're very helpful, and Kansas is up by one with 3:05 left to play in overtime. Perfect. Also handy: fake calls from work, or pretending to adjust someone's TV settings—put on a sports station with scrolling scores, while all the time adjusting imaginary scenarios on a "buddy's" remote, and voila! Minutes of unscrutinized score watching. Maybe you finish with, "Samsung always has adjustable db's, but I would suggest going with your factory defaults ..." Ha. Genius.

Be careful of being greedy, and beware of obvious pitfalls. Do *not* duck into a dark room for a quick peek. That bright mobile screen acts like a spotlight on a guilty face. When caught, don't plead innocence at this moment. The "I was just checking the weather for tomorrow to see if it was okay to go antiquing, because I was going to surprise you" line won't work. Also, don't make sounds, happy or otherwise—your wife or girlfriend knows that you're probably not that upset that Elliot didn't get the lead in the school Christmas (a.k.a. holiday) pageant. You're upset that Drew Brees just fumbled the ball.

On the other hand, some people are just asking for it. I know someone who scheduled her wedding on what turned out to be Game 7 of the Stanley Cup final. And her fiancé's team was in it. The wedding party was conspicuously absent for most of the evening. She still talks about it. Her husband, though? He played by the rules. That is, he didn't get caught.

77 SHOOTOUTS IN THE NHL ARE GOOD

It took a while for me to decide if I liked a shootout for deciding an NHL game. I wanted to pan it right away, simply because I didn't grow up with it—that's what age does. Ever hear old people say, "Well, back in my day ..."? Remember how you would mock that phrase? Well, guess what? I've become Dana Carvey's grumpy old man. *Well, back in my day, we didn't have shootouts; you'd play until your eyes started bleedin' and your heads would explode. That's right, games that went forever with bloody eyes and heads poppin' right off your shoulders, and that's the way it was, and WE LIKED IT!* So, I was patient and now I have made a decision.

I don't like shootouts.

Hockey, being a team game, needs to have a team resolution, not a skills competition. I understand the excitement over the skill set necessary to make some of the moves you see in a one-on-one situation (I'm a fan, too), but to me, it is something that should be reserved for an all-star competition and not a real hockey game. I don't think I want to see an NBA game decided by the best one-on-one competition. I mean, strength is an important part of the game. Maybe each team should send out their strongest guy and see who can bench more.

Now people have some negative feelings about the "minigames" played in NCAA football and the CFL, but you get a winner and you're still playing the team game that got you to that point. In the NFL, you can still achieve a tie, even with the new rules. Take a look at an NFL sideline when overtime has expired and see the faces there. Most players and some coaches have no idea what's going on. Why? Because ties at this level of sport are unacceptable.

Major League Baseball doesn't have ties. That's right, baseball. The sport that plays 587 games in a season, has doubleheaders, and will keep playing literally until the lights burn out. They still keep playing extra innings until a winner is found.

The NHL is tinkering with formats during overtime that will hopefully eradicate the "showdown" feel to ending games. I know this also makes some feel uneasy. I'm not convinced three-on-three is the answer, but you would sure as hell get an end to a game pretty quickly, and it would still revolve around a team game. The team that could read plays, set up on D, find the seam, jump on opportunities—that is, *play hockey*—would win. One way to look at it is to note that if anyone tried the neutral zone spin-o-rama that Linus Omark used against Tampa in a shootout a few years ago, and there was a defenceman on the blue line, it wouldn't have been Omark going 5-hole that would show up on the highlight reel. It would be Omark getting crushed.

But to me, it still sounds "entertainish." I love the four-on-four overtime format, as the scoring chances are numerous and the pace is fantastic. Now, if you eliminated the "loser point," teams couldn't dog it for a point—play to win or you get nothing. But, of course, you will get the argument that the so-called loser point has kept many teams, and therefore cities and fans, in the race for the playoffs longer. And for the NHL, this has been a good thing, but that's just another way of saying we should reward mediocrity. And who's to say that if there weren't a loser point on the line, those teams wouldn't play differently. Perhaps better.

I still say end it. This isn't high-school intramurals; it's pro, and pro sports are ruthlessly competitive. I often think to myself that if I lived in ancient Rome, I would be giving a lot of thumbs-downs. They probably had a version of the shootout for the Roman Colosseum, but you wouldn't want to see it. It's never a good idea to bet on the Christians either. If the elite gladiators were the Harlem Globetrotters of the day, the Christians were definitely the Washington Generals.

And if I am sticking with my Roman Empire analogy, then I give the NHL shootout the thumbs-down. Now, more wine, and where did that Thracian slave girl go? I think she liked me.

78 *YOU DON'T NEED A BACKYARD RINK*

This is so stupid that no one would actually say it. So why point out that it's wrong?

Because too many of us *act* as though it were true.

It may not seem like much, and maybe you've never made one before, but a backyard rink is the stuff Canadian life is made of. Some of my fondest memories as a kid were either watching my dad making our rink or, when I got older, helping him. It isn't even so much about the skating or the hockey games that would follow, but the almost Zenlike moments that exist in the art of creating it—the steps that it takes to make it resemble a recipe from the pages of a master baker. You have to get the right temperature, the right amount of water—and do you use the tarp method or the traditional packing down of snow for your base? All of these considerations make you feel like you are the creator. It's quite the adrenalin rush for the average man. (Is using the word *creator* here insinuating that you are, in fact, God? Yes. And on the seventh day, when the frozen universe is created, you will say, "This is good." And you will rest, probably with a nice rye and ginger.)

How about boards? Oh yes, a must in my tradition, as there will be hockey, and hockey of every kind. There are different kinds? One of my favourite kinds of hockey on a backyard rink is the always-hilarious one-on-one, have-to-stay-in-your-end, boot hockey with a tennis ball. Banking shots is a must, as the instability of your footing is great for laughs and, naturally, humiliation. Staying on your side of centre is perfect because should the ball misfire and end up resting near the middle of the ice, the icy spinout boot race is on! Invariably, somebody is grabbing the other guy, pulling him down for a mock fight as the ball rolls toward one of the nets. Guys can kill hours doing this; just ask my friend Robbie "Knob" McVicar. If there ever were a Boot Hockey Hall of Fame, he wouldn't be inducted for his goal scoring but perhaps for the best laugh while fake fighting in the history of the game.

What about lights? Absolutely, there should be lights on a rink; after all, afternoon games are great, but the big boys come out to play at night. I would say the only flaw in night games is the inadvertent shot over the boards and into the snow. Remember how badly it sucked skating off the ice in the dark and using your sticks like chopsticks, trying to dig out a puck from the snow? I believe now, technically, that is a delay-of-game penalty.

Penalties in rink hockey? One year we built in a penalty box. Why? Most years, at one end of the rink, we had this huge heavy piece of wood that was like a barn floor. We supported it with steel bars and hammered it deep into the lawn. After flooding and the inches of ice that were eventually laid, it was in there, baby! It was the "bodychecking area." Really, what it became was the "charging area," the "hitting-from-behind area," the "cross-checking area," and the prime-time "fake fighting area." These infractions were governed strictly with penalties enforced immediately. I believe it was thirty seconds in the box for all incidents. As I recall, Knob was in there quite a bit and complained very frequently, including accusations of unfairness as I never received any calls whatsoever. So what? It's my rink. I make the calls. I was the Soviet Union in the 1970s.

So get outside and make a rink. You're building more than an ice surface—you're creating memories. (That may go down as the cheesiest thing I have ever said. You know what? I think I am now sitting thirty seconds in the penalty box. I hope you're happy, Knob.)

79 IT IS AN EASY CHOICE TO NOT TAKE STEROIDS

So, let's say you're a 19-year-old athlete. You've been recruited by a huge NCAA program. We can assume that you live and breathe sports. Let's say football. You've dreamed of football since you were a small child. All your hopes are devoted to football. Football has given you the best opportunities you've ever had, and football is where you expect the rest of your opportunities to come from. Football is going to allow you to buy your parents a new house. Football is going to make you a star.

Now someone comes along and tells you that the way to keep going in football is to take juice.

Would you do it?

For me, I can honestly say I don't know what my answer would be. I am being honest. I know what the optics are and I would hope that my own God-given talent and hard work would get me drafted, but to say I would immediately say no would be a lie.

Remember, you're someone who has gotten where you are

by doing whatever it takes to win, including sacrifice. You know there are risks, but guess what? There are risks every time you step on the field. You're always one hit away from having your knee destroyed. Is taking steroids any different?

I'm not saying it's a good idea. I'm just saying that if you've devoted your whole life to making it, staying clean is a lot harder than just saying no.

Is it cheating? Yeah, it's cheating. But if you've spent your whole career looking for every small advantage, maybe it doesn't feel like cheating. Especially if you look around and see other people doing it. According to the Youth Risk Behavior Surveillance System study, 4.9 percent of male high-school students in the United States and 2.4 percent of females have used anabolic steroids at least once in their lives. And that's students in general. You can bet the percentage among athletes is much higher.

But a look at those numbers will tell you that it doesn't work. Even if it's just 5 percent of male students who take steroids, only a vanishingly small percentage of those are going to make it. It varies from sport to sport, but it's consistently below 0.1 percent who have a career in the show. If you're a marginal player looking for a small nudge to get over the edge—and for the most part, those are the guys—juice *might* get you where you want to go. But it almost certainly won't.

Still, there is more to steroid use than just competitive advantage. I was once told by a Dallas-area high-school football strength coach that at times it wasn't even about guys getting bigger for football, it was just about non-athletes wanting to look "good." There is an enormous amount of pressure on our kids to be one of the gang, whether it be to get a spot on a team or to make sure your arms look like something from *Jersey Shore*. In the old days, all guys needed to do was a lot of bench-pressing and risk a shoulder injury; now they risk heart damage and growing breasts.

In every movie we see today, when the guy rips off his shirt, what do you see? Does he look like the cool movie idols of days gone by? Burt Reynolds, Clint Eastwood—when those guys took off their shirts, yeah, they looked bigger and more athletic than most of us. But they still seemed like normal men who looked after themselves. Now even the average underwear model is ridiculously ripped, while movie stars are built like NFL linebackers. (I have to admit, though, that what I see is a bunch of guys who don't drink beer. That's right. If you want shredded abs like that, you're not at the pub putting down pints of Guinness with your buddies. And if I had to choose between a six-pack and a pint, you know which one I'm going to choose.)

But forget for a minute about the kids who have ab envy. When it comes to kids looking for an advantage on the playing field or on the ice, it isn't enough to simply repeat the mantra, "Just say no." That doesn't explain to the young individual why taking HGH and PEDs is a path that could lead to destruction. I honestly believe that exposing players such as Roger Clemens, Rafael Palmeiro, and Lance Armstrong is good because it shows the eventual annihilation of a career and a reputation. But do our youngsters feel the same way about a Von Miller or Shawne Merriman? As long as there is a grey area, the taking of steroids is still a choice. There are pros who got away with it (Andy Pettitte, Jason Giambi), some who still do today, and always athletes who believe they can. We need to put a stop to steroid use, and it starts with kids.

80 EVERY TEAM NEEDS A GUY TO STAND UP AND GIVE A SPEECH

A lot of people think that inspirational players are usually the ones who are verbally the loudest—let's call them rah-rah guys. The common perception is that these individuals are an important part of any team's makeup.

If you think this, you are wrong.

What teams really need are individuals who lead by example. Sometimes, the loudest guys can be your worst. Maybe you're picturing heartfelt speeches given by coaches or players to inspire the team—and moments in the dressing room that demand Knute Rockne– or Herb Brooks–style performances in order to motivate a team toward success. Give me the guy who doesn't cheerlead but takes the team on his shoulders, on the ice, field, or court. Those are the players who are needed in the dressing room.

It's about leadership, and about being an instrumental presence for a group that is trying to find success as a team. You might ask, who are these players? They are Saku Koivu—what he meant to the Montreal Canadiens as captain after overcoming non-Hodgkin lymphoma, and what he currently means to the Anaheim Ducks, is immeasurable. Peyton Manning doesn't say all that much, but when he does, it's usually with touchdown passes. Jonathan Toews is a prime example of everything you would want in an athlete and team leader, plus he does it all with class, humility, and a dignity that is infectious throughout the entire team. Before his career is over, I think he may go down as one of the all-time greats. Would Wendel Clark like to get through life without talking at all? Maybe. But when he was on his game, he could make every player on his team stand a little taller and fight a bit harder.

There are those who believe it's the coach's job to motivate. I would suggest that the motivation from coaching lies within their ability to teach and develop already good players into great ones, with the ultimate goal being a championship. Over-the-top speeches are great, but you can do it only so many times. Ironically, the toughest coaches aren't the yellers. They are tough by challenging players mentally and emotionally. If the only tool a coach has is his voice, the room can, and will, eventually tune him out.

Maybe *Rudy* was a great story for Hollywood and made for an excellent movie, but the always-intense, constant cheerleading from a subpar teammate isn't inspiring—it's annoying. I once went to a dinner in Hamilton where Rudy was one of the main speakers. An hour into his sermon about "what one needs to do to be successful in one's life," he had only gotten to breakfast and how to cut bananas into your cereal. The blathering intensity with which he spoke was just too much. I went outside to smoke a cigar. Surprisingly, I ran into two university coaches who had also stepped out. "Too much?" I asked. "I would've cut him," replied the one coach. Ha ha ha ha ha! That was awesome! When I went back inside, I believe he had started hour two with "how to sleep." Shut up, Rudy!

81 SOME TELEMARKETING SERVES A PURPOSE

No. Absolutely not. There is nothing good about telemarketing. How some goof thought that invading the privacy of other people's homes by a stranger accosting you over the phone to purchase something you never inquired about is beyond me. It doesn't matter what the product, service, or charity is—don't call me! Is it pure greed on the part of those organizations that use this method? I think it is. The thought process probably went something like this: "Hey, we can simply reach the entire population to sell our product and never leave the office. They *have* to pick up the phone and even if we irritate and inconvenience 98 percent of the homeowners, we might get 2 percent of that business. Two percent we never had before." How arrogant. They don't care about us, and it's harassment. It's stalking. It's anything but good.

But what about charity, Mike? Let me give you an example of something that just happened to me an hour ago (and is the chief reason I'm writing this chapter now). A (region-censored) police association has been calling my house. I donated to them a year or two previously. Since that time, they, plus maybe ten other "charities," have bombarded my house with phone calls. All times of the day. Every day. Like a lot of you, my phone at home has blocking features. Mine has the ability to block thirty numbers. I long ago reached capacity. Thirty numbers and it's still not enough! We have a family member battling cancer; we're unfamiliar with some of the necessary phone numbers that we need to answer, so we have to pick up. My wife picks up the phone. She hands it to me …

VOICE ON PHONE: Hi, Mike.

ME: Yes, this is Mike.

VOICE: Hi, I'm calling from the [region-censored] Police Association and …

ME: Let me stop you right there. I've asked to please be removed from this list, as we get a million phone calls a day and we can no longer …

VOICE: Yeah, right. That's impossible.

ME: Pardon me?

VOICE: I'm pretty sure you're not getting a million calls a day. That's impossible.

ME: You have to be aware of how many times you have attempted to contact me because …

VOICE [NOW WITH A RAISED VOICE AND ARGUMENTATIVE]: There are 365 days in a year and …

ME [CUTTING HIM OFF]: Are you seriously chirping me in my own home??!!

VOICE [NOW JUST TALKING OVER ME AND BEING COMBATIVE; IT'S 9:30 SATURDAY MORNING]: But you …"

ME: May I speak with a supervisor? Please!!
VOICE: Yeah, sure. Whatever ...

Now, I go on to speak with the supervisor, who sounds like he didn't want to give me the time of day. Sort of the "yeah, what is it now" kind of attitude. I state my name, tell him what just happened, and he really doesn't seem overly concerned. I then restate my name, explain what I do for a living, and tell him I will completely blast this charity coast to coast on TV and for a whole week on radio. I will make it an act of retribution for all of us who have been verbally confronted in our own homes without any consideration for our privacy. Silence. "I understand, sir. I'm very sorry." I simply say, "Listen to the recording of what just happened. I don't think you want this person representing your charity." Then I tell him I won't blast the association because of one imbecile. "Do you wish to have your name removed?" "Yes, thank you," was my response.

As I'm writing this, I'm still stunned by the event. Also at the time of this writing, I'm praying they don't call again. If they do, you'll know. Along with the name of the association. Jesus!

82 *THERE AREN'T ANY REASONS TO GET ANGRY WHILE DRIVING*

There aren't any reasons to get angry while driving, except that all other drivers are IDIOTS! Wow, do I drive mad. I drive every day like I'm in *Tokyo Drift*, minus the bad acting and hot chick who loves me despite my anger, as well as her evil Japanese mafia boyfriend who is also a bad actor. Has everybody just forgotten the rules of the road? Are people just making the rules up as they drive? And if you're like me, do you wish you had a James Bond–like car in which you simply press a button and a machine gun lays waste to the vehicle in front of you? (I'll even go so far as to admit that I often pretend-hit an imaginary button on my dashboard, see in my head the car burst into flames, exploding into pieces as I drive through it, and then make a "movie quip" out loud in the voice of Sean Connery like, "Next time listen more closely to your driving instructor.")

Why are people so intent on driving in the passing lane? It is called that for a reason, but people will sit in it forever, oblivious to those who drive up behind them, clearly visible in their rear-view mirror. Ahh, the mirror! You think "Johnny One Speed" ever looks? No way. But, I am not an advocate of those who tailgate Johnny just to see if numbnuts will move. He won't. Don't get me wrong, I hate Johnny, and his sister Jenny, and especially Grandma One Speed. I hate the whole family. Apparently, they are a big family and getting bigger.

And who buys vans? I hate vans. I get a chuckle out of the names they have for these road-blocking vehicles to make them sound sleek, regal, or space age: Odyssey, Grand Caravan, Town & Country, Sprinter, and Quest. Let me rename them: Loser, Fatty, Sight Blocker, Natalie (a tribute to the character from *The Facts of Life*), and The Anvil. Yes, it has its function for the larger families and those who play sports and need the space, but couldn't you get a nice sport utility instead? Can't afford it, you say? THEN WALK TO THE GAMES, YOU TRAFFIC BLOCKER! WORK HARDER OR YOU SHOULD HAVE STAYED IN SCHOOL, YOU RITA MACNEIL OF THE ROADS! Like I said, I'm an angry driver.

Fast driving doesn't bother me. I like the speeder. Let's call him "Hans." He's confident and knows where he's going. "Ahhh," I think to myself, "so refreshing to see a guy who's got his priorities straight. And just look at his car: modern, expensive, and in great condition. Why, I bet Hans is wearing cufflinks. Now that's a driver." But guess what? You know he's going to run into someone from the One Speed family. So I yell, "Hit the machine-gun button on the dashboard, Hans! Kill 'em! Kill 'em all! Bwa ha ha ha ha ha ha!" I know, I really have to find a peaceful hobby.

Maybe if I could just plead to those who aren't confident when they drive, or who are the gawkers, the daydreamers, and the selfish: Just think to yourself, "If I'm not passing anyone, *ever*, then I should never be in the passing lane." Not that hard to remember. Because if you can't, don't be surprised when you wake up in a plastic-covered room, bound down on a gurney with what looks like Saran Wrap, and you see me standing over you in coveralls and latex gloves, saying quietly and close to your face, "Do you know why you're here?" And when you glance around the room and see pictures of vehicles stuck behind your car, you'll be overwhelmed by a powerful sense of fear that paralyzes your entire being, freezing your ability to talk. "I know you don't know," I'll whisper, "and that is why you have fallen within my code."

What? What happened? What was this chapter about? Oh yeah, driving ... yeah, that's right. It's fun for the whole family!

83 IT'S AN EASY LIFE BEING A PRO ATHLETE

You know what they say. Do something you love and you'll never do a day of work in your life.

Bullshit.

Assuming you beat the odds and actually manage to become a pro athlete, it may *look* easy. Playing a game that you've played since childhood, receiving a huge paycheque, being adored by millions of fans? If anything goes wrong, it's not life or death. A missed free throw is a lot less anxiety-inducing than a missed mortgage payment. Let in a soft goal, and now you're sitting on the bench? Hey, buddy, just about anyone would take that ahead of getting laid off. You just lost a big game? That's right, a *game.*

I get it. And there is no doubt about it, being a pro athlete is a privilege. No one is holding a gun to these guys' heads, forcing them to be millionaires.

But that doesn't mean it's easy.

The fact is, apart from the truly elite players, most of the guys in the show are not *that* much better than the guys in the minors, or the ones who don't make it at all. Think of the can't-miss prospects who never crack a pro roster—what happens there? Or think of the guys who go on a tear for a year, then disappear. How can you score 50 goals one season, then dry up?

Lack of talent is not the problem. Nobody doubts that Alexandre Daigle had talent. But there was something he didn't have, and that something is hard to develop and maintain.

Ever see NHL players working out at Gary Roberts's gym in the summer? If you think that's not hard work, I don't want to know what you do for a living. Most guys work out like that. Guys like Sidney Crosby or John Tavares may not be hulking tough guys, but they are absolute beasts in the gym. That's pure work.

And if you're a player like that, you need to be that strong, because you've got other, ridiculously strong guys trying to knock you off the puck, game after game. And cross-checking you in the face. And chirping at you. You've got fans in other cities holding up signs announcing how much you suck. You've got reporters criticizing your game. Some nights, you must be tempted to say, "Screw this!"

But if you even think it, you're done. And if you're not one of those elite players, if you even think about thinking it, you were probably never in the show anyway. To be there, you've got to be relentlessly focused. So focused that when someone knocks your teeth out, you get right back out there for the next shift. Don't feel like it? Don't worry, we've got plenty of other guys ready to take your spot.

Does that sound easy?

Now, try keeping that focus as a young man, only recently moved out of your parents' (or a billet family's) home. You've got money and fame. And you've got a lineup of young women throwing themselves at you. I know, it sounds terrible. But we all face temptation. So imagine what it is like facing a minefield every single day. All the while trying to stay focused.

(And let's be honest, any time you hear of a pro athlete and a woman, how many times do you blame the player? Like, almost every time? And, what about women pro athletes? Are they targeted as well? Yes, and I've seen them tracked down by other women. Not to perpetuate a stereotype, but I was at an LPGA tournament and was surrounded by young, stunningly attractive women. I turned to a buddy in the clubhouse and said, "Look at all these chicks?!" He nodded his head slowly and said very quietly, "They're not here for you ..." Oh. What I saw that afternoon was a little shocking, as young women circled some of the tour players looking at them in a manner similar to a leopard stalking its prey. Weird, and it proved my naivety in this circumstance.)

And it gets worse if you're a pro. People everywhere take their mobile phones with high-end video cameras, record your every move, then send or sell the footage to news agencies moments later. And those agencies will find a way to make you look like a terrible person while you were at a restaurant, in a parking lot, or walking down a school hallway talking to your child's teacher—whether it is all taken out of context or not.

How about the constant pressure of friends and family who think it's fair that you give them money, because after all, you "owe" them for everything they have done for you. (I always wonder, who in their right mind thinks that they are owed money because of someone else's sacrifices to achieve success simply because of a shared last name or neighbourhood? And yet it happens.) Speaking of family, let's not forget about the substantial time away from spouses, children, parents, and siblings that can be really trying for those who search for normalcy and balance in a life that is anything but normal.

And there is another harsh reality. People never realize how short the stay in the show can be for a pro athlete. It doesn't last forever. Fewer than half of the guys who make it to the NHL last more than a hundred games. In fact, fewer than 20 percent of the players who are drafted play two hundred games. The average NFL career lasts 3.2 years. How about the NBA? The average there is 4.8 years. So, after the career, or "cup of coffee" at the pro level, then what?

If you think the threat of having everything you've worked for your whole life being taken away at any moment is easy, well, you're wrong.

84 *CAMPING IS FUN*

Camping might be the absolute worst.

I'll never go. I don't want to. Do you ever wonder if the homeless walk by and think, "Are they mocking me?" There is nothing more unappealing than the thought of sleeping on the ground in the year 2014. It's not adventurous or getting back to nature or health inspired—it's a crap vacation that makes you wonder how our forefathers even made it as far as they did. Speaking of which, after the years of travelling across the great frozen and mountainous Canadian terrain, after facing hypothermia, frostbite, starvation, and death, did pioneers not think, "Maybe we should turn south?" I love my family tree, but would it have killed someone to say, while perhaps eating the frozen remains of Grandpa, "You know, I hear Florida is nice."

What is so fascinating about sleeping in a tent? If there is anything that we have learned from our experience of trying to survive in North America over the last two hundred years, it is that sleeping underneath canvas gives you the most chance of dying. It doesn't protect you from bears; cold; fat, falling drunken guys; or escaped mental patients with goalie masks and chainsaws. People always say, "But the air … smell the air!" There's air at resorts, too. In fact, most places I have been have air. Seemingly, it's everywhere.

What about the notion that food tastes better outside? I happen to think it does as well, served by a waiter, poolside, with a wine list and a hot hostess. What about beans on a fire, Mike? What about the beans? I'm sure they're great and very much enjoyed by the other hobos as you wait to jump onto the next moving train. Toasted marshmallows? I'm not 10. Graham crackers? I'm not poor. What about swimming? I own a pool.

"You can't get a better sleep!" Oh, yes you can. It's called a mattress. You know where you can get a mattress? Everywhere, including resorts, hotels, and my favourite: a cottage. Now cottage life is a different story. God invented cottages and anyone who owns one is a genius. Both the beauty of the outdoors and the comforts of the indoors are rolled into one. No canvas and beans here—we're talking steak and red wine overlooking the lake. You want adventure here? No problem, just go inside the cottage and flip on the Samsung 65-inch 1080p LED flat screen and turn to satellite channel 468 (it's Discovery).

Some camping enthusiasts will even go in early spring or late fall (personnel from ministries of parks and recreation call them "missing"). You want to camp in the snow and become a "mansicle," that's up to you, but the sane mind says, "Sleeping in snow under canvas, bad." You want nice, fresh oxygen? Go to Vegas. They pump fresh oxygen into the casinos 24/7 and you get free drinks as long as you keep gambling. Adventure, fresh air, excitement … all the elements you search for in camping minus the beans, mosquitoes, and gory death.

If you like the weekend jaunt into the woods, do it when you're in your early twenties. At that point, you don't know any better, and if your camping mate is a pretty girl, trust me, I get it. But renting a cottage, staying at a lakeside resort, or going on a tropical and all-inclusive vacation—that is the life for me. You know who still does portaging? No one. They're all dead.

85 *RUSSIAN HOCKEY PLAYERS ARE ARROGANT*

Bloody Russian hockey players, with their tinted visors and their attitudes. They never want to talk to the press. And when they do show up in public, it's always with *other Russians*. Outrageous! Who do they think they are? Coming over here and having the audacity to snub us and cower from the limelight that we so kindly thrust upon them! And now that I think about it, some of those Czech players have pulled that same routine. You rarely see a kid from Saskatchewan or Alberta or even Minnesota try to get away with the ol' "I'm not talking to you" routine. It's pretentious, that's what it is!

Or that's what I always thought. But I came to an uncomfortable conclusion after my experience broadcasting my morning show from Ufa, Russia, during the world junior hockey championship in 2013. From the moment we arrived in Ufa, having travelled from Moscow, it was obvious that we had become extremely isolated culturally. On the first morning, taking a cab to the arena was an experience. A man in his fifties stood by his taxi as we tried to explain where we wanted to go. He stared back, no smile, no expression, and shrugged his shoulders. Then we did what all stupid North Americans do, which is say the exact same thing again in an accent—one we thought sounded Russian. "Vee be vantink to be goink to da areeena." He drove away. We're idiots. A younger Russian man who observed the Cirque de So Stupid took pity on us, motioned to get in his car, and said, "Arena hockey?"

We piled in and I sat in the front seat. "Well," I thought to myself, "here comes the mending of the cultures as I, Mike Richards, will now converse with a local and everything will be fine!" I smiled and looked at him. He smiled and looked at me. I pointed at a tall building and he smiled and nodded at me. As we drove, there was less smiling. Less pointing. More driving, then silence: painful silence. If this were the international version of *Gay Blind Date*, I realized that I would be bombing. Roger Lodge would be making sarcastic comments at this point and embarrassing balloons with funny comments like "there goes the hot tub" would be popping up everywhere in the uncomfortable silence.

Later that day in yet another cab, I didn't bother even trying. Not once. And then I started talking English to my co-workers in the back like the driver wasn't even there. And then it hit me. I'm doing what the "damn Russians" do in North America. I didn't really talk to the workers in the arena. If the staff around the press box were speaking Russian, you would just walk on by. When you left the arena, you would leave by yourself or with others from your work group only. No conversation for you!

Then I got it.

The Russians, Czechs, and players from elsewhere weren't conceited. They were isolated. It's not that they don't want to talk to you—some can't. And those who can speak some English don't want to look stupid. They are all proud people and they are men: That combination means they would rather not embarrass themselves. Now, that's not to say that there aren't exceptions (hi, Alex!). It would be like saying all North American players are affable and humble. Scientifically, I think we can all concur that every culture around the world will always have a percentage of their population classified as "dicks." But does it vary that much from culture to culture?

During the lockout, Joffrey Lupul headed over to Russia to play in the KHL. A lot of players did. And a lot of guys came back pretty quickly. Lupul was philosophical about it, though. He said something like, "Oh, if it's hard for me to play in Russia because of the language barrier and culture shock ... then maybe it's hard for Russians to play in the NHL because of the language barrier and culture shock."

As a side note, that night and every night for two weeks in Russia, I sat at the bar from 11:00 P.M. to whenever, and with the help of my Russian brothers, some of whom looked like extras from *Eastern Promises*, I learned as much Russian as was humanly possible. My name became Misha Yakoshev. "Walk a mile in their shoes" was a lesson never learned in a more poignant fashion. My mind changed forever.

86 *IT'S A GOOD IDEA TO TANK TO MOVE UP IN THE DRAFT*

Tank Nation: stupidest idea in sports.

I can't help but think those who came up with Tank Nation have never played a competitive sport in their lives. If you want your team to lose, here's a secret you need to know: No team loses on purpose.

Actually, who does lose on purpose? How would you feel about a lawyer who lost on purpose? Or a musician who played wrong notes on purpose? How about a plumber who deliberately left leaks?

The thing is, *it doesn't even work*. Remember Fail for Nail? How's that working out? Remember the scandal in Ottawa when the Sens allegedly tanked to get teenage phenom Alexandre Daigle? Ouch! (Especially when they could have had Chris Pronger in the two-spot! Or Paul Kariya at four ... or Saku Koivu twenty-first.)

Okay, maybe I shouldn't have mentioned Pronger, because for the most part, the idea that one pick—one 18-year-old kid—is going to turn a team around is just false. Have there been players so significant that they could single-handedly change the fortunes of a professional franchise? Yes, but historically the odds are miniscule. The reality is that smart drafting, good scouting, strong front-office management, excellent coaching, and developing from within make up a far superior and longer-lasting methodology than uttering, "Hey, let's all lose so we can get the 18-year-old!"

Plus, how would you like to be a team leader and be asked to lose so that some kid who has never played a game in the league can come in and do your job better than you? Translation: You suck.

It also begs the question about the ideals that fans have about professional pride. If you are a pro sports team that sits in the middle of the pack in the standings, how do you convince those who have sacrificed most of their lives to get to a pro level and have been wired to succeed and conquer to just simply roll over? Not only cease to compete but maybe lose for a sustained period of time? Tank Nation suggests that pro athletes and those who run those teams have no problem morally "taking a dive." It doesn't say much about how these fans perceive the moral character of those in pro sports either.

But these so-called sports fans aren't very savvy or knowledgeable about how the world of sports works anyway. If you are talking about a team that has faded, a team that has played poorly for several seasons and has bottomed out to the point where there is a belief that a "sports messiah" is going to bring salvation and change their fortunes with the wave of a stick, the passing of a ball, the turning of Gatorade into wine, you might wanna find a new team.

The other thing that is just so unbelievably hypocritical is that those fans who complain about their team's results, screaming that "they have no heart" and "don't care about the fans," have no problem demanding that their team lose on purpose. How are you ever to trust an administration that would make a decision so devoid of character as to lose on purpose? Could you honestly believe that in the future they would have nothing but good intentions for the success of the team?

It's not like I think teams haven't tanked in the past to improve their draft position. The NBA has been accused of being the worst offender. The implementation of the lottery has helped to a degree, but there are those who are still accused. So you have to ask, even if the team was successful in throwing away its season and reputation, and acquired the player in question, did it ultimately work? Well, for Cleveland, they got LeBron. He tried his best, but he had no one else. So he left for South Beach. Cleveland tanks again and acquires Kyrie Irving. As of this writing, the Cavs are out of the playoffs with no championship in sight, but they have won the draft lottery again (after also winning it in 2013) and are poised to select Canadian phenom Andrew Wiggins.

I'm not arguing whether tanking happens—it clearly is attempted. But in my opinion, when it comes to the philosophy of Tank Nation, I simply wouldn't want to be associated with those who have mismanaged their business so poorly that they believe underperforming and losing on purpose is the best way to move forward.

87 *MEN DON'T CRY AT MOVIES*

I think that, mostly, men don't cry very much. Women certainly cry more than us and we are usually the source of the crying in the first place. But emotionally, we are wired differently than women. Many of the fairer sex will cry for extreme happiness (i.e., weddings), baby showers, and heartfelt greeting cards. They will also cry if there is a significant or dramatic moment in life, like a sunset, two old people holding hands across the street, or a Bell long-distance television advert. For men, it's different. I'm not crying. I can't and I won't. We certainly aren't crying at movies.

Well, most movies.

Every once in a while, guys, you're allowed to cry. For those moments, I have created Mike's Man Movie Rating—the MMMR system. You're welcome.

The ending of *The Shawshank Redemption.* I have seen this amazing film ten times and always say the same thing: "Okay, big boy, when Morgan Freeman comes walking down the beach in Zihuatanejo and sees Andy working on the boat, don't well up, pussy, don't do it ... Waahhh! Damn it!" Every single time! But how can you not? Look what the two buddies went through to get there: the beatings, the corruption, the rape, and crawling through poo! Damn it, men, it's okay to cry. Just not in front of other guys. MMMR: *Watch it alone.*

It's okay to cry during parts of *Braveheart.* For men, it is an emotional roller coaster because of the confusing mix of love scenes (blech) and excellent scenes of blood, head/hand chopping, and revenge. You just have to ask yourself if you're crying because of the lost loves of William Wallace or because he dies in the end. Best not to admit anything. Just be glad the Scots keep killing the English and Longshanks gets screwed. MMMR: *Shared male watching is possible, but no looking at the other guy.*

Brian's Song. This sports classic about Brian Piccolo and Gale Sayers is in the Mike Richards Man Crier Hall of Fame. There is no penalty or flag for this one. But we all know that, as men, we can be susceptible to the emotion of the "sports crier." Therefore, *Field of Dreams*, *The Natural*, and *Rocky* may induce some welling up. The emotions caused by climbing to the top against all odds *and* winning or losing the girl is more than we can take. But there is a caveat to this genre: I'M NOT CRYING AT *RUDY*! (In fact, I'm not watching it.) MMMR: *Watch sports movies on a treadmill. If you're watching *Rudy*, run super-fast to cause the earth to go in reverse rotation, thus going back in time so you can cut Rudy from the Fighting Irish and prevent this story and movie from ever happening.*

All wartime movies are also in the no-flag category. *Saving Private Ryan*, *Schindler's List*, *Von Ryan's Express*, and *The Great Escape* are all weep-if-you-want films with no penalties or Brendan Shanahan–like disciplinary judgments. I'll even say

The Green Mile can also be included in this category. (Just don't admit that the mouse part at the end makes you cry.)

So cry if you want to, but please watch these movies with extreme caution. Don't be seen. Don't express your feelings, you Clay Aikens, because that is grounds for a revocation of your Man Card. And remember that there is always a Steven Seagal, Jason Statham, or Bruce Willis marathon playing on some channel somewhere. Nothing wipes away tears for a man like a little neck-snapping. Thank God.

88 BEING A FATHER DOESN'T CHANGE HOW YOU WATCH SPORTS

This isn't so much an argument as it is a fact. Becoming a father will change how you watch and feel about athletes and sports in general. It's amazing how the circle of life does catch up with you at some point. Most of us remember our fathers taking us to the rinks at ungodly hours on winter mornings to watch us skate on our ankles and fall down. (I should also mention the very special moms who have done the same thing.) The memories are vivid for us, but sometimes we fail to look at it from our parents' side—the weight of those memories and how they must resonate with them as they watch us get older. It isn't until you become a parent yourself that you finally realize the gravity of these special times and moments. You understand that your son (or daughter), your child, the apple of your eye will always be just that. Regardless of the level of sport that they play, the amount of recognition, fame or money, the player wearing number 18 for the Leafs, 12 for the Flames, 86 for the 49ers, or 26 for the Yankees is somebody's son.

In 2009, Jesse Lumsden was playing his first game with the Edmonton Eskimos. Jesse was as promising a football player as Canada has ever produced. He had quick feet, was fast, and had a great football IQ—skills he came by honestly, as his dad, Neil, was a collegiate and CFL star. Unfortunately, the injury bug haunted Lumsden's career both north and south of the border. In his first game with his new team, playing at home in Commonwealth Stadium and trying to revive his career, Jesse's shoulder was dislocated on a hit from Siddeeq Shabazz. As Jesse lay on the ground in obvious pain (again), I wasn't wondering who the Eskies would bring in; I wasn't considering how they would change their offence; I was heartbroken for his dad, Neil. I thought of the kind of pain a dad sees in his son, watching his boy go down. Again. These are dad thoughts, not sports-morning-man ones. On the other hand, I also know how proud Neil is of his son—now retired from football, Jesse was part of the Canadian bobsled team in the Sochi Olympics.

In a recent NFL game, while watching a simple running play, I heard a terrible scream from one of the offensive linemen. I immediately thought, "What if it was my son who just made that sound?" Being a dad never stops. We see these athletes as super-gifted, super-rich gods, but they're each somebody's boy. Archie watching Peyton and Eli on the field, Walter watching Wayne on the ice, and Richard Verlander watching Justin on the diamond—they all have the same thoughts: son first; athlete second. After the career ends, no matter how storied or glorified, they are still like they were from the very beginning: your child.

My son, who played on the defensive line for St. Mary's High School in Calgary, is now 23 and graduating from Wilfrid Laurier University. I have accepted that my dream of his holding the Vince Lombardi Trophy over his head in the Superdome, after winning the game MVP, is probably over. But considering Jordan is the nicest young man, who is very happy, with a great sense of humour, and a wonderful ability to make others smile (plus he stays close with his old man), he is the best thing I have ever done. He is my Super Bowl.

89 *EATING DINNER SHOULDN'T LAST ALL NIGHT*

I'm always running into this phrase: "dinner and a show." Well, here's the thing: Dinner *is* the show.

I've never understood why people would go out, wolf down some food in a restaurant, then head on to something else. What's the hurry? Dining shouldn't be the mere act of *feeding*. Where's the conversation? The gossiping about people? The sarcastic quips about other diners or the wait staff? Man cannot live on bread alone. As George Benson once sang, "Give me the night!"

Now, if you want to go to a performance, a movie, or a play, I say do it first and eat after. The late dinner is my favourite thing. And the best place for the late-late dinner? Vegas, baby, Vegas! I remember going to see Jerry Seinfeld at Caesars Palace and then having a fantastic meal at The Venetian, Thomas Keller's Bouchon. Perfect steak and frites, big bottle of Cali red, and, yes, more talking. Unfortunately for the servers, I had been drinking and I had just seen Seinfeld for two hours, so the staff got a lot of this: "So, what's the deal with mussels? If they're so strong, why do they get caught so often? Ever notice the coat-check guy doesn't really do a lot of checking? It's more sitting. The only thing he really checks is his watch, waiting for the moment he can get the hell out of there and someone else can watch his coat." I got a lot of looks from the waiters like, "Oh look, he's doing Seinfeld at 2:30 in the morning. How fun for us ..."

The same philosophy should be followed in your own home as well. Inviting people over for dinner is one of my most cherished activities. And even if it's the "come over around 4:00 P.M. for fancy cocktails and hors d'oeuvre," I do expect most to make it until at least 1:00 A.M. And yes, I prefer people to stay over. That way I can spy on them when they go to the bathroom. (*Aha!* Just wanted to see if you were paying attention.) But seriously, I've seen some people so fidgety around 9:00 P.M. that I start to wonder if they're on parole. "Well, we've got a big drive ahead of us, so ..."

So *what*, exactly? Attack birds start dive-bombing cars after 9:00? You're afraid of zombies? Your superpowers start to wear off? And just how far is a big drive? The other side of the city? Do you live two provinces away? I can't believe you didn't fly in? I hate those kinds of guests. They're definitely the "dinner and a show" people.

It's also nice not to have "the clock" constantly over your shoulder when presumably you're socializing with people you just don't get enough time with. If you rush a night out, it feels like you are saying, "Oh, we would love to go out to dinner with you and Sally, but really I can only see your worth to us socially as about an hour and a half. Two hours tops. Then you have to leave. And not with us. You're on your own."

Take your time. Make the night about you, and not just the eating or show—that's only a part of it. So if you come to my house or out for dinner with me, be prepared. You're going to be in it for the long haul, because I think you're worth it.

90 THE MOST WONDERFUL TIME OF THE YEAR

Andy Williams sang about it, so you know what I'm talking about. Decorating trees with your family, having turkey, dreaming about Santa Claus, perhaps even chestnuts roasting on an open fire. Ah yes, "the most wonderful time of the year" is Christmas! Right?

Wrong. It's March Madness!

Yes, the NCAA basketball championships that propel CBS television viewing right over the moon, catapulting its ratings past *NCIS*, *Survivor*, *The Voice*, America's Dumbest Assholes, and all the other ungodly shows that have denizens of trailer parks all over the States screaming, "Jed! Get the ketchup for the popcorn! Mama's shows are on!" Oh sure, in Canada you'll always get some "loud rock" blabbering, "Nobody likes college basketball!" Although the numbers are not as enormous as they are south of the border, they are significant, and the increase could be due to the fact that there are more Canadian kids playing NCAA at a higher level than we've ever seen. During March Madness 2013, twenty-seven Canadians were on the court, including featured starters like Kelly Olynyk, Anthony Bennett, Kevin Pangos, and Nik Stauskas.

College basketball from morning to night; all the bands and cheerleaders; play-by-play announcers losing their minds—if this isn't paradise, I don't know what is. And the gambling … ohhhhhh, the gambling! I believe at one time, when I was still playing Pro-Line, I would be filling in the dots with pencils so frantically and quickly that the tickets were literally bursting into flames. My third-biggest single Pro-Line win came during March Madness, a nice $6,400 courtesy of the magic of Pro-Line Ties. And God. Don't forget God.

I love the drama of March Madness, and, of course, there is nothing more dramatic than the plays, and mistakes, made by young men giving it their all during the most pressured event of their lives. It's honest and it's raw. The emotion during these weeks is almost beyond compare with anything else in North American sports. I think the only other equivalent in terms of sustained drama over that period of time would be events like soccer's World Cup, the Olympics, and other world/international tournaments.

It is also yet another excuse for men to gather for long periods of time to ridicule and mock each other in front of the TV, with extra time for insults and bad language. More cocktails, beer, and wine for those who watch this magic unfold. Which also brings up another issue: bucket-list items regarding March Madness. Among these would be going to the Final Four, including the championship; a regional tournament trip; and maybe the biggest wish of them all: March Madness in Las Vegas!!! Can you imagine? Even Caligula would watch me in Vegas and say, "I'm not doing that!"

Waking up and making wagers at 8:00 A.M. while wearing a white tuxedo jacket with Penélope Cruz on my arm … drinking champagne and laughing! Now that's the life for me.

Shut up. It could happen.

Some of the greatest coaches in sport conduct this athletic symphony of chaos. The integrity shown during these weeks makes me feel like there is still true effort given in sports in this day and age of capology talk, prima-donna-player rumours, tank teams, and what have you. No computerized bowl games here; no polls or journalists telling us who they *believe* is the top team. You live for the day or go home. The first mistake could be your last, and that could cost you and your team an entire season. If you'd rather roast your chestnuts over an open fire, I don't know what to say.

91 *YOU GET OVER YOUR FIRST TV CRUSHES*

False.

Anyone who says they don't think about their first TV crush is full of it.

I do. And so do you. Not that you *obsess* over an individual whom you saw on a screen thirty-five years ago and never actually met. (What are ya, Manti Te'o?) What I'm talking about is that "flutter" you get when you hear the name of a certain actress, or the show she was on, or when a picture of her appears on the TV.

Admit it. I just saw a book cover with a picture of Valerie Bertinelli on it. The star of *One Day at a Time*. That Valerie Bertinelli. The one I fantasized about asking to a prom, movie, or dinner date, and then always back to a car for heavy making out. That Valerie Bertinelli. The girl I went horseback riding with on a Caribbean beach, skydiving with in Hawaii when we ran into the Bradys, and who was the co-pilot on my very first solo flight.

But sure, there were other crushes that come to mind. Susan Dey, who played Laurie Partridge on *The Partridge Family*, was another of my imaginary torrid love affairs. Wow, she was something, especially when I would meet her after one of their shows. I would joke around with Keith, trading hair secrets, and Danny was always annoying, but that didn't stop Laurie and me from making out on the family bus! Ohhh, those were good times.

I think I also had a little something for Marcia Brady, but she was a little annoying—too perfect. We would break up a lot. Greg was pretentious and Peter was always prying. I also think the fact that the family had AstroTurf in the backyard freaked me out. Marcia, Marcia, Marcia!

What about *Charlie's Angels*? If you didn't imagine stuff with Farrah Fawcett, I just don't know who you are any more. That hair, that body, and that face influenced what girls in malls would look like for the next five years. In this particular fantasy relationship, there wasn't a lot of hand holding, walking on beaches, or talking. It was, ummm, you know. And a lot of it.

I watched *Mork & Mindy*. I watched it really good. Too much probably. For her. I always wanted to do a remake of that show with Pam Dawber called Porkin' Mindy. I just looked it up: too late.

The fact is, most of us have those crazy first crushes from TV and it's okay that they still have a little zing to them. I just pray that this conversation doesn't bring up names that just don't feel right, like Aunt Bee, Mrs. Cleaver, the Bradys' maid Alice, or Miss Hathaway from *The Beverly Hillbillies*. Come to think of it, Elly May Clampett had a thing going on with the jean shorts—what we now refer to as Daisy Dukes. And while we're on the subject, Catherine Bach as Daisy Duke? Boing!

I once heard a guy talking about Alyssa Milano and crushes. Now, she is hot, and we're all aware of that in the guy club, but it got a little uncomfortable when the *Who's the Boss?* reference came up. What was she, 11 when that show began? We were supposed to be talking about TV crushes, not about guys who would eventually drive windowless vans.

So hold on to your feelings because they are yours and yours forever. I know I was just saying to Valerie how funny it is to talk about this subject. So you'll have to excuse me, because I'm just going out to a car to make out with Val. Don't tell Laurie Partridge anything about this or Keith will kill me.

92 PROFESSIONAL ATHLETES DON'T NEED TO HAVE FUN

Fun may be the most underrated factor in anyone's life, let alone that of the pro athlete. And outside the dressing room, it is a bigger factor than most give it credit for. I think many feel that even the word *fun* has a childish, unprofessional, or frivolous connotation. Fun is the means of achieving happiness and it's a reflection of the enjoyment one has; in the context of a team, that fun is shared. Ever been up close with a professional team that isn't having fun? You can even tell in the morning skate!

So, in professional sports, what is considered fun? Answer: winning. Winning equals fun. Obviously, easier said than done, and I think teams that still find a way to enjoy each other and the job they have during tougher times give themselves a better chance to be successful. How is this done? Different ways, but one of the most common is to alleviate pressure. By this, I mean pranks. Now keep in mind, a lot of pranks executed among young males truly are only funny if there is danger involved. You'd like to think otherwise, but it's true, thus the common phrase from many parents, "What were you thinking?!" In fact, I'll give you a great scenario that actually happened, and I don't believe it has ever been in print before.

My late uncle, Guy Kinnear, started as trainer for the Marlies in 1967, and in 1969, he became the trainer for the Maple Leafs for the next twenty years during the Harold Ballard era (known to some as The Dark Ages). When the Maple Leafs visited Los Angeles during the 1970s, especially over the winter months, the newspaper headlines would shout things like, "Maple Leafs in Hollywood!" Was it fun for the team? Yes. But, as Paul Harvey would say, "Now, the rest of the story ..." A player who shall remain nameless told me once that as "the boys" were fooling around in the pool at the hotel, they noticed "Gunner," Guy's nickname, had dozed off poolside. The players thought it would be funny to wake Guy up, and egg him on to dive into the pool. They then proceeded to the shallow end of the pool and got on their knees. Well, good ol' Gunner, hearing the encouragement, got right up and dove headfirst into the pool! And, as Gunner surfaced, exposing a slightly bloodied bald head, the team erupted. Bwa ha ha ha ha ha ha ha ha! Gotcha! Now, Gunner never went to Harvard, and considering there was no paralysis, it goes into the books as a legendary gag.

What workplace exists successfully with the absence of fun? It's no different in the world of professional sports, and the release of tension is important. I think *fun* also comes with a sense of pride when you achieve a level of excellence because of the dedication to the sport; the execution of your game plan as laid out by the coaching staff in practice; and a mutual respect you have for the team, the coach, and the organization. Not all fun is related to the "pie in the face" routine or shaved eyebrows in the middle of the night, but there is no question that teams that have no fun go nowhere. Of course, you could have fun and stink, but your career probably doesn't last as long. I wonder if the Jacksonville Jaguars have fun?

93 *IT'S ALWAYS BETTER TO WATCH A GAME LIVE AT A STADIUM*

If the game is big enough, it then becomes a story to tell others that "you were there." On New Year's Day 2014, I watched the Winter Classic between Toronto and Detroit at the Big House and it was spectacular. But as I watched the frozen flakes swirl into the 105,000 frozen faces, with many donning ski masks, snow goggles, and parkas, I came to the conclusion that my seat was better—in front of the toasty fireplace, watching the big screen, surrounded by friends, food, and booze, with a short walk to the washroom. I know. That's terrible, what I just said, but I'm now at the age when I don't want going to the bathroom to feel like a scene from *The Walking Dead*.

Big stadiums in general make for big television events. To look among the sea of humanity is always a glorious shot and there are many of them during the broadcast. The announcers will tell you time and time again how the throngs have travelled from afar to witness this magnificent spectacle, like they were the 80,000 wise men. The many strategically placed TV cameras will be discussed, as well as the number of people watching at home. The only thing that's not talked about is that these few chosen ones who are lucky enough to be present at the game, in section Z, row 547, seat 1018, can't see ass from those chairs. You can't see what team has the ball. You can't see what sport it is they're playing. Add to that the potential danger of extreme cold and drunken students—the vomit, the urine, and the semen—I think I'll stay at home in the air conditioning. (Those last things may exist as well in my house but at least the shower's close.)

The funny thing is that as you get older, other factors that you would have never considered when you were younger become troublesome. "What time does the game start? 8 o'clock??!! That's outrageous! Don't they know what time people go to work?!" Another issue that causes trauma is parking. It is the great divider, especially among the 35-and-up demographic. If you're under 35 years of age it's, "Let's stay up all night!" Over 35 and it's, "I'm not paying *that* for parking!"

There are some sporting events that I still think are worth the inconvenience. Playoff games in any sport are the best. Do or die, there is no tomorrow, putting the season on the line: All the clichés are there because they are true. (Although I'm sure after losing an important game, there still is "a tomorrow." Never has the world stopped, but we get what they mean.)

So go to big events if you like. I'm happy for you. And if you need me, I'll be by the fireplace, with a rye and ginger, eating bacon-wrapped scallops and making sarcastic remarks to Katherine Webb as we both laugh. After A.J. McCarron's loss to Oklahoma in the Sugar Bowl, she decided she no longer wants to go to the big game. Besides, she told me, "Do you know that game started at 8 o'clock?!" I hear you, sister, I hear you.

94 BASEBALL PLAYERS ARE TOO CONCERNED WITH THEIR IMAGE

You can see how some guys might get self-conscious. The sun is shining, thousands are gazing down on you from the heights. Millions are watching on TV, so you'd better be ready for your close-up. Remember, you've got to think about your image. I mean, your brand.

Hey, sounds like the perfect time to adjust your gitch.

Seriously. There is more scratching and adjusting going on out there on the diamond than at a rave in a leper colony. Why are these guys so itchy? Is it the sweat, the standing, or the pine tar? Are the uniforms too tight or mysteriously covered in burrs? Has the game become so boring that scratching has helped to make the game more interesting? And the amazing thing to me is that there is no area seemingly out of bounds for those doing the scratching.

Okay, let's just say what it is: the groin area. The adjustment, the pulling, the tweaking of the meat and two veg, sack attack, marble movement, checking the coin purse, calling Jimmy Johnson, ordering McNuggets, shipping the package, waking Peter, moving the tent pole, picking berries, and shaking the wedding tackle are all a part of what we see during every baseball game. Are baseball players even aware that they resemble those guys at every Italian wedding I've been to when the boys go outside for a smoke?

Now what about the spitting? Baseball happens to be the kind of sport that allows you to continue a bad habit while actually playing the game. Chewing tobacco or "chaw" has been a long-time tradition in baseball. Over the years, mostly because of health issues, baseball officialdom has tried to steer its players in other directions. Not that I didn't enjoy the constant spew of black juice being sprayed all over the field and batter's box like Linda Blair after a night of tequila poppers, but it was decided that tobacco use must be cut down. Sunflower seeds became a popular alternative, but instead of dark-coloured expectorant all over the field, you now have a perpetual barrage of seed shells that players release like a salt truck on the 401. Certainly healthier, but the diamond after every game looks like the kitchen floor of Colonel Sanders after he tried to pronounce the word *statistics* with his mouth full of peanuts.

Facial tics, hat tugging, neck twisting, eye blinking, and shirt pulling are also constants in baseball culture. Why? I believe it's because of all the lulls in the game. In hockey, you can spit, but adjusting the twig and berries during a shift is not advisable and hard to do. The gloves alone would make it hard for even Peter North. Football has some issues, but the players seem to hide it better. They're more into ass slapping, which is higher in style points and at least more sexually satisfying.

So please, baseball, let's try to clean up the aesthetics of the game. You're starting to look like the cast members of *The Facts of Life* when they run out of Wagon Wheels.

95 *PARKING AT A MALL ISN'T THAT HARD*

What percentage of people do you believe have good driving skills? Maybe 70 percent? Sixty percent? Fifty percent? Now, how many of those have good parking skills?

I wouldn't trust most of the people I encounter in a parking lot not to pee their pants.

Parking at a mall is probably the worst thing you can do on a Saturday afternoon. Or any afternoon. Or morning. Or night. Anytime. Parking is something you should do only if you are comfortable hating your fellow humans. Because that's how it's going to end.

Have you seen the faces on some of these goons? They look more terrified than the B actors you see in all of those paranormal-activity movies. By the way, how many of these odd occurrences are we to believe have happened? It seems like every week now. What's the next movie? Paranormal Activities: The Loblaws Years.

The parking-space lines are too close together for actual parking. Who wants to be close to other human beings? Not me. I don't even like charity. Ever stand too close to another person on a subway, GO train, or any other form of public transit? I feel like I'm rowing beside Charlton Heston on a slave ship in *Ben-Hur*.

As I kid, I wondered where carnivals got the idea for bumper cars. Now I know. How many times have you come back out to a lot to find your car scratched, dented, or dinged? With no note left. What would you do if you caught one of them? Oh, I know! I would have to borrow from the movie *Law Abiding Citizen*, with Gerard Butler. Sure it's a little over the top for a parking-space accident, but imagine if that were the penalty for being a douche at a mall parking lot? You'd hear a lot of, "No, I'm sorry, after you." "No, no, I insist, after you." "Oh please, you were here first." "That is so kind of you!" "It's my pleasure."

I've seen fights. I've seen yelling—lots of yelling. I've seen my brother snap at a 150-year-old Asian woman who almost ran us over trying to get a parking spot. And that's the other "game show" element that comes with this territory: the senior citizen. I love them. We're all going to become one, if we make it there, but in the parking-lot scenario, they're like the *Star Trek* extras who wear red: They're getting it first. And if they don't, they're causing it. I cringe when I see a silver-haired person, head just above the dashboard, putting the car in reverse. It's like watching a drunk baby, with a walker, chase a balloon off the edge of a cliff.

It seems easy, but it's not. Just do what I do and park far away from others. Stay away from people. I believe that's what Sissy Spacek's mom told her in the movie *Carrie*. Speaking of Stephen King, remember *Christine*? Now there was a great car to park.

96 *LET'S GO HIKING!*

For the life of me, I'll never understand the fixation that some people have with walking in the woods where there is difficult footing, chance of death, and no bar facilities.

I've heard the phrase, "Let's go exploring!" That's not exploring. You're not Magellan. Where you are walking has probably already been discovered, especially if it's an hour away from Lake Louise. Yeah, we got it: Alberta. Thanks, Ponce de León, but you really can't claim Golden, B.C., as your own. What you are actually doing is wrecking an afternoon that could be spent lounging by a pool with cocktails, or relaxing in front of a big-screen TV while watching the excitement of college football, or sitting in a cozy bar telling waitresses fantastic fabrications about yourself.

I often heard this when I lived in Calgary: "Take safety precautions in Banff, as there have been bear sightings and some hikers have been killed or maimed during their walks. So please be safe." I have a safety tip: Don't go walking where bears live.

This safety message has been brought to you by The Mike Richards Self-Preservation Society, sponsored by Wisers. Wisers: Stay in the neighbourhood you know.

Have you seen the losers who walk with ski poles? Are you shittin' me? You need a walking apparatus to make this hike happen? It either says you are not very adept at this walking thing or the trails you are taking may not be for you. They look ridiculous; then again, they think hiking is fun. I've seen goggles on these nerds. Walking goggles? Look, I get that most of these people have never played a sport in their lives, so this is a chance at "athletic redemption." I can just imagine the conversations at restaurants. "Harry and I love to go hiking. We did ten miles of trails on our last eco-vacation ..." Okay, two things: One, anyone who would sit with people in a restaurant who start talking about hiking trails has terrible friends. If they are the most interesting people you know, time to broaden your horizons. Two, "eco-" anything in a sentence means it can be replaced by the word "sucks." "Let's go to Costa Rica for an amazing eco experience!" No. I'm not going. "Let's go to Costa Rica to an all-inclusive resort for a sexo experience!" Yes. I'm going.

Sometimes in my mind, when I hear the word *hiking*, I envision the Alps or the Rockies, snow caps and rushing waterfalls. I also see pulling myself up a mountainside and swinging across the cliff face to safety, while trying to outrun John Lithgow and his band of criminals. And then it hits me—I'm not thinking about hiking. I'm thinking about Sylvester Stallone in *Cliffhanger*. See? Hiking with pole-walking, goggle-wearing losers—not fun. Escaping from villains in the mountains while making out with Janine Turner—lots of fun. It's not even close. So don't even try.

97 SMALL ACCOMPLISHMENTS IN SPORTS DON'T MATTER

If it weren't for small sports accomplishments, none of us would ever golf again. It's always great to think about those big personal moments from our pasts, and it is always assumed that those moments are significant, but the reality is, it's the smaller accomplishments that always stick with you. It follows the same logic shared by many coaches that I have spoken with over the years. As much as the championships are cherished, it's the losses you never forget. It doesn't matter at what level, or at what age: A hard loss burns forever. The same goes for the small sports accomplishment. You always remember the moment.

Remember your first goal in hockey? Of course you do. You remember the time and probably the team you played for and the team you scored against. You were probably 5 or 6 years old. How about getting your name in the local paper? It might even be the same story featuring your incredible goal versus Mac's Milk. The first time you were able to pitch windmill style in softball. Not easy, and, honestly, not a position or sport I really played, but I still remember when the pitches stopped going over the backstop or bouncing off the ground. It feels like yesterday, but it wasn't. I was 12.

Winning your first running race of any kind might be the greatest feeling in the world when you're a young kid. Boy, do you feel invincible. You feel like a superhero, like Superman or Batman, but don't let that little "gem" out of the bag or your first race will be followed by your first beating as a "nerd." The first time I caught a really deep football pass thrown by an adult was a day I'll never forget. Jim Fletcher was my gym teacher in grades 6 and 7. He showed up late in my primary schooling, but, man, what a finish. He was a good athlete. I mean a really good athlete. He pushed me to do great things, and a lot of what I did athletically later in life, I attribute to him. One late recess, while I was playing football, he took the ball and screamed, "Go deep!" I ran as fast as I could, and of course my buddies ran right after me. I still remember the release of that ball and the sound it made so high in the air. *Fizzzzzzzz* was the sound that perfectly thrown spiral made as it started to rocket toward the ground, but something was different. I still had to keep running. It was coming down, but just ahead of me! What??! As I continued to sprint, I reached out in front of me without breaking stride as the ball zipped right into my outstretched hands! I still remember my buddy Robbie McVicar (remember "Knob"?) yelling, "Holy shit!" as I lunged into the imaginary end zone! It had to be at least 50 yards. And it still feels like yesterday.

Golf might be the greatest example of all. Hack away for hours with ample moments of frustration, anger, despair, and hopelessness—and then it happens. A chip in, a long drive, or a crazy putt. *Boom*, you're back, baby! For a lot of guys, it's the first time they break 100, 90, or 80. (If you've broken 70, piss off, nobody likes you anyway.)

And how could I not acknowledge those guys who fill up the parking lots (and the bars) of suburban rinks across the country. The guys who play beer-league hockey in the hope of capturing a faint hint of the glory of playing hockey as a kid—the smell of the artificial ice, the clattering boom of pucks coming off the boards, and the thrill of sniping one over the goalie's shoulder (then daydreaming about it at work the next day). So if you sit around a dressing room a couple times a week with half-naked guys who call themselves the Mighty Drunks, or the Master Debaters, the Fussy Puckers, the Punch Drunk Imlachs, the Cunning Linguists, or the Ice Holes (I could go on), my hat is off to you, sir.

98 *THERE ISN'T A TOUGHEST POSITION TO PLAY IN SPORTS*

There are many demanding sports. Some have a tremendous endurance factor, where the ability to stay strong is of the utmost importance. The new wave of athlete has tended to slide down the path of extreme sports. Triathletes, extreme fitness people, and cyclists certainly can boast about the difficulty and physical sacrifice that it takes to participate in their respective events. Traditional sports like hockey have a toughness that is undeniable, plus a physical side that makes players some of the most physically fit athletes in any sport. The game moves fast and so does the decision-making. Basketball takes a balance of all athletic skills and rolls them into one game. But to me, there is a toughest position to play in sports and it has just two letters: *Q* and *B*.

In some corners, the argument is that it's not physically demanding to play the quarterback position. Not compared to what other positions and sports require on a sustained level in order to compete. But that would be simplifying what the quarterback position is all about. At the pro level, the requirements for playing quarterback are staggering. Some QBs make it look easy. And you could argue some aren't the greatest of athletes. But this is not an argument about the greatest athlete in a sport; rather, the most difficult position to play.

Here is your job. You gather ten men (or eleven, depending on your country) to coordinate a complex play that will unfold in a matter of seconds, maybe less. The average pro offence could have literally hundreds of plays in its playbook based on particular formations, but it's reasonable to think that on a game day the offence could have as many as sixty ready to go. As you line up behind your over-300-pound behemoths, you direct your outside receivers who are 50 to 60 yards away from you by using a series of verbal directions or signals, and a sophisticated cadence that is followed by the snap of the ball.

Previous to this action, you must take in at a glance the eleven players on the other side of the line of scrimmage—among them are 275-pound monsters who want to kill you, plus the four other 250-pound beasts behind them who are always angry, while watching the movements of the four or five ripped psychopaths who are jumping around trying to stop your pass, bury your receivers, or on occasion join their friends in trying to kill you. In that moment, you have to read what they are likely to do and come up with a plan to evade them.

When the ball is snapped, you must make immediate decisions on which receiver is getting the ball *and* make sure you throw it. Perfectly. Now, focus. Remember, you are being hunted down by a wall of angry humanity, who on average will give you only three seconds to make this decision. Having fun yet?

The precision of a Peyton Manning is literally a thing of beauty. Tom Brady, Joe Montana, and the other maestros of this position truly are artists of athletics, intelligence, decision-making, and organization. You must be a highly functioning human being to play QB. Oh, and by the way, everybody will weigh in on every win and especially every loss. You are in on every play. EVERY PLAY. You are the target on *every play*.

And if your receiver runs the wrong route, it looks like your fault.

If your offensive line sucks, you got it. Your fault.

I've heard people say, "Stop worshipping them! They're not gods!" That might be true. But I swear, every time I watch *The Ten Commandments*, I think, "Isn't that Dan Fouts parting the Red Sea?"

99 *CHRISTMAS LIGHTS ARE FUN!*

If Christmas is a time to celebrate the birth of Jesus, then why did we let Satan invent Christmas lights? Ho, ho, ho? Shut up, Christmas lights. I know you're mocking me. Every year it's the same thing: unravelling the ball of green-wired mess, checking to see which lights still work, and not remembering which connections go with which strand. And here's a surprise—half the lights don't work! I just bought some of these last year! Pieces of garbage! Then the wife is calling through the window:

WIFE: Are you putting the lights on? I can't see them. They don't look right.

ME: Arrghhh! Shut up, woman! Get off my back!

WIFE: You said you wouldn't use bad language outside this year! I can hear you swearing!

ME: I'll kill you!

WIFE: No. I'll kill you first!

And what about the number of lights, styles, bulbs, and shapes these sparkly globes from hell come in now? Those icicle ones look stupid. I don't know who thought those look Christmassy. Of course, they were designed and made in a country that doesn't have snow, or celebrate Christmas. What the f*%& are LED lights? Are they blue? White? What are "warm," "cool," or "pure white" LED lights? White is white, but not in this freak-show, over-the-top, Clark Griswold, Jesus-a-palooza, Christmas light extravaganza. And don't get the wrong white bulbs! Oh, you are asking for trouble!

WIFE [THROUGH THE WINDOW]: I thought you went to get white light bulbs.
ME: I did. I just got back.
WIFE: Those are the wrong white ones. I don't like those ones. You know that!
ME: I don't like you!
WIFE: Well, I don't like you.

Now they have ones that come like a fishing net. A meshing. Seems like a pretty good idea, except they come in a weird square shape. What on my property is perfectly square? So, you do what everyone does—you pull on it. *Fizzle, pop, fry, zzzzzzz! Holy shit, I almost electrocuted myself! What the hell!* It's usually at this moment when the carollers come a-wassailing. "Joy to the worl—" "Shut up! Shut up, you happy, 'up with people,' Disneyfied, animatronic freaks!"

WIFE: Who are you yelling at? I hear bad language.
ME: I almost got electrocuted!

WIFE: I don't think the mesh ones look good. There's too much white.

ME: Serenity *NOW*!

Whatever happened to the old multi-coloured, straight-across-the-eavestrough, up-in-an-hour, standard Christmas lights? Perhaps a floodlight or two, and, if you dare, a red or green one? Oh, I miss those days. Simple, festive, and traditional. You want your property to look good and you don't want to be the crap house on the end of the court. My neighbour Walt always does such a nice job with his house. Damn that Walt!

100 *IT'S EASY BEING ME*

I think at times there is a perception that the road I travelled must have been easy and that it has always been fun. The show I have been able to do is fun, don't get me wrong. I can't count the number of times in my life when people have said, "I can't believe this is your *job*!" But the show you hear and see now is the end result of a very rocky and sometimes almost impossible journey to get *Mike Richards in the Morning* to air. From the moment I started in this business, I always had dreams, but I spent the majority of my years trying to have just *one* person understand what it is I was trying to do. The reality is it took eighteen years.

I started at 1050 CHUM in 1986. That's right! One big circle in twenty-eight years, and now it's my third occasion on the 1050 dial here in Toronto. That company was always CHUM, and in my heart, 1050 will always be related to Allan Waters, his son Jimmy, and the family that many of us will always cherish. If it weren't for those people in the early days, I'm unsure if I would have continued in a business that started to change in the mid-1980s from what it had always been, creative and imaginative, to regimented and controlled. The consultants of the time made sure everything was calculated. What was said, when you said it, and, more importantly, what you were playing. Forget about announcers choosing their own music to reflect the personality of their shows, the consultants wanted you to play specific music at a specific time to ensure you were getting the "right" audience. This strict world wasn't for me, or for long-time radio vets, and I had to figure out what I wanted to do in the business.

After doing my midnight shift at CHUM, I started listening to "air-check" tapes of midday jock Gerry Forbes. He was good and funny, but he was able to do this in a strict, cardboard cut-out of a format called Favourites of Yesterday and Today. (Don't get me started. I know, I know.) Gerry and I became radio partners down the road, and he is one of the best friends I've ever had. No one knows more about radio than Gerry. But after this period of time, I would go from Toronto station to Toronto station as a "funny sidekick." At times, it was really fun. The show that I did with John Derringer at the FAN 590 in Toronto was a fantastic time! Our program director (PD) at that time was the legendary Bob Mackowycz, Sr. (I have to say "Sr." now because of "Jr."!) We put out a lot of stuff. But as always, there were changes. More people who didn't get it. And once again, I was changing stations.

I have spent a lot of time out of work. From '91 to '94, '98 to '01, and '02 to '04. During the '91 to '94 period, I started a comedy service called Headline Comedy. It was the start of the comedy bits I do now, my understanding of doing impressions of local personalities for cities I was not from, and learning about production (very important). But the stations still changed. The

PDs still stared at me like I was an alien and I was still not doing the gig I imagined.

And then I got a call from an interesting fellow named Kevin Usselman. He wasn't a boss or in management. He was a co-host of an afternoon show at the FAN 960 in Calgary. He had heard Paul Romanuk and me when the FAN was the TEAM and wondered if I would do bits on their show.

"For what?" I asked.

"Keg certificates," he replied.

I don't know if people realize it, but that conversation has brought me to where I stand now. The PD called me and we talked. Kelly Kirch was the only guy up until that time who "saw what I saw." In *Matrix* terminology, he was the only one who saw me as "The One." The accomplishments at the FAN 960 were enormous, and hitting number 1 as a sports radio station on the AM dial can all be credited to one man's confidence in me: Kelly Kirch.

Fast forward to today and TSN 1050 and the televised version on TSN 2—it's light years from where I started but still a project in the works. I have big plans for this show, and as I have always said, "I'm just getting started." I still get weirdos, complaints, naggers, and goofs who hate everything, don't understand "it," hate me, think I'm disgusting, and wish me the worst, but the harsh reality is this: They've lost. No more vacuous program directors or those who tried to blackball me. The show has won. It will continue to grow, and for that, I thank all of you and owe you my life.

ACKNOWLEDGMENTS

I would like to acknowledge those who supported me in this business and have helped me get to where I am today. Without them, I'd be working at Ed's Store of Filthy Books. To Gerry Forbes of CJAY 92. Nobody could find a better or more loyal friend in any lifetime. He understands more about the real workings of radio than anybody on the planet. Calgary is lucky to have him and I am lucky to call him my friend.

To Jeff and Julie Lumby. For all the support I received from a business standpoint, no one saw more of the bad times than these people. They literally kept me upright. I call them Mom and Dad even though we're basically the same age. It's creepy to others, but nothing is more accurate.

To those who probably don't realize what a profound impact they have had on my career just because of how talented they actually are: John Derringer, Paul Romanuk, Bob Mackowycz, Sr. (I love Jr., but I'm talking about his dad here), Stephen Brunt, Peter Maher, Pierre McGuire, and Bob McCown (honestly, without his persistence in getting me live on air in the early days of the FAN 1430, I'm not here; let's face it, he knows talent).

Special thanks goes to FAN 960 program director Kelly Kirch in Calgary. The only guy in Canada who had the "stones" to put me on the air solo, regardless of what anyone told him. He was the first programmer who truly had my back as a morning man and as a friend. If you like *Mike Richards in the Morning*, then thank Kelly Kirch: He is singularly responsible for the success I have today.

Also a huge thanks to Nick Garrison from Penguin Canada for taking a chance on me and believing I could write a book that didn't contain pictures (or centrefolds), and to my literary agent, Brian Woods, who, to put it simply, is one of the nicest guys you could ever meet.